Chaos and Grit

Chaos and Grit

Barbless Bits & Little Chits

Phyllis Burgess

Singing River Publications, Inc.
Ely, Minnesota

Published by:
Singing River Publications, Inc.
Ely, Minnesota
www.singingriverpublications.com
218-365-3498

Photographs by the author
Book design by Dorie McClelland, Spring Book Design

ISBN 978-0-9789870-9-1
Printed in Canada by Friesens
First edition

12 11 10   01 02 03

To my beloved husband, Jim
(I did this for you, dear)
and
My precious daughter and son-in-law,
Pat and Paul Krieg

Acknowledgements

First of all, my gratitude to my readers, who definitely are responsible for the survival of this column, Chaos and Grit, for more than five decades. Your encouragement, your support, your acceptance, your assistance—what can I say? You will never know how much your notes, letters, telephone calls, comments when we met, have meant to me. Even a sentence written on your subscription reminder card which you enclosed with your payment was a treasure to me. As our masthead says—"The nicest people in the world!"

And to Chris Moroni, my publisher, whose professionalism, enthusiasm, drive and encouragement guided me through this unknown, frightening world of book publishing. She had her hands full, believe me, but she never wavered and was firm, but always kind and thoughtful. Without her annoying deadlines, this project never would have reached fruition. I knew that, but balked, nevertheless. She is a gem.

Then we have Fran Silverberg, with her calm approach, her efficiency, her support and her excellent suggestions. She is a veteran at this book publishing and she realized that it was an uncharted course for me and quietly led me through. Another gem.

Family, of course, is a given. Everyone should have a family such as mine. Loving, helpful, supportive, so, so patient! My sister, brothers, nieces, nephews, cousins and their spouses and families. I am truly blessed.

Chaos and Grit

Chapter 1

He was not just good-looking. He was downright handsome—my Jim. Well aware of his good looks, he was very particular about his appearance. He was always clean shaven, except during deer season, when it was traditional for the men in his hunting shack to grow beards during the season. He would chide friends if they neglected to shave for a day and try to shame them into being more fastidious about their appearance.

After his barber, Jack Yernatich, retired, it seemed that no barber could cut Jim's hair exactly right, and he would painstakingly explain to the various "new" barbers just how he wanted his hair cut, breaking it down to each side, the top and the back of his head—but he never seemed quite satisfied with the results. At age eighty-eight, he still had a beautiful head of thick hair, and he was proud of that fact. His clothes had to fit just so, the cuffs of his pants extending to a certain point at his ankle; he kept Nancy Yapel busy adjusting the length. The shoulder seam of his shirts and jackets had to curve around a certain point at his shoulder. He appreciated nice looking clothes.

Jim always looked—and acted—far younger than he was.

When out hunting and camping, he could keep up with men half his age. He was at hospitals and clinics all the time during the past six or seven years, and the nurses, female doctors and other female members of the hospital staff constantly commented on how young and handsome he looked, to his great delight. They would say, "I just looked at your chart, and there is no way you are (such and such) years old!" Jim loved it. Wherever he went, he would strike up a conversation with a nearby person and the topic of age always seemed to surface. "How old do you think I am?" Jim would challenge, and, of course, the answer was always ten or fifteen years younger. Jim enjoyed their astonishment and disbelief when they found out his age.

Jim was a friendly person who visited with everyone. Through the years, new neighbors would not even be completely moved into their new home before Jim was there, introducing himself, offering his help—and assuring them that he would be there to assist them or lend them anything they needed. He loved people. He would come back home, excitedly telling me about the "new people." He had their whole life's history. A neighbor across our tiny bay, but blocks from us, commented at Jim's funeral, "Jim was one of the first to welcome us when we bought our cabin. We enjoyed his little visits that he made from time to time. Such a nice man." He would take daily walks, stopping along the way to chat.

He always had "to help." If he saw a neighbor involved in a project, Jim would hurry over, often with suggestions of a better or easier way to accomplish the work. I think that might have been why they sometimes refused his assistance—more often than not, it had to be done Jim's way, which, of course, was the only "right way."

He loved children and would sit and observe them and study them, smiling and calling my attention to that "beautiful little girl— look at that smile!" or that "handsome little boy—have you ever seen such beautiful eyes?" Children adored him, and those who knew him would scurry over to him and crawl up on his lap, cuddling and sitting there contentedly. They gravitated to him, sensing how much he appreciated them. Jim was always so proud of the way the children would seek him out in a whole room of adults.

Jim approached every day of his life with an intensity and vigor that could not be matched, even when he was in failing health. There was no halfway with him. He lived (that is not a typo—it is meant to be an "i") to be outdoors, to hunt and to fish and excelled at whatever he did. When he was devoting every minute of his spare time to fly fishing, he was not satisfied until he went the extra mile. He got numerous sports magazines and actually studied some of the articles and it was not long, of course, before he advanced to fly tying. He set up a work bench in the back of the newspaper shop for his fly tying equipment and all the hooks, feathers, animal hair and other paraphernalia that this tedious, exacting hobby involves. With his usual demand for perfection, he was meticulous about his product, discarding more flies than he kept, even though I thought very single one looked wonderful—if insects and bugs can look wonderful. Authentic would be a better word. When he caught a trout on one of his flies, he was ecstatic and he would make sure that Pat and I saw the fly that "did the trick." He was not satisfied until he got Pat involved in the fly tying. His area of trout fishing soon extended almost to the North Shore, over trails that could not even be dignified by the term, "road." With his usual enthusiasm and zest for life, he loved every minute of it.

After a number of years of reading about the phenomenal trout fishing in Montana in his sport magazines and having checked out every stream from here to the North Shore, he decided to extend his trout fishing activities. "Go West, young man, go West." All three of us headed for a Montana vacation. He was more excited than a little boy at Christmas when he saw the shops that he had read about in his magazines and got to visit with some of the well-known fishermen in that area. A Paradise on earth for him! He was at the trout streams before dawn and stayed there until dusk. These were different streams from what he was accustomed to fishing (actually, rivers), and he decided after the second day, that he needed a guide. Luck was always on Jim's side and he got one of the best known trout fishing guides in the area. Life could get no better than that!

A restaurant in West Yellowstone would cook your fish for you—just bring the fish in and tell them what time you wanted to eat. Jim found out about this restaurant on the first day of our stay, so every day he would bring in his prize catch. As the waitress carried his fish to the table on a platter, wending her way through the whole restaurant, everyone would exclaim loudly at the size of Jim's fish, even standing up to get a better look at the beautiful trout, just like a picture. They were, indeed, exceptional—gorgeous and huge—trout. Jim was absolutely ecstatic and basked in the admiration of the other diners at his fishing skill.

On our second trip to Montana, we, of course, went to the same restaurant to deliver fish just as impressive as the first year, and the red-headed waitress remembered Jim. They had become good friends during our first visit. He asked her if she liked trout, and when she enthusiastically said that she loved trout, he promised to catch one for her the next day if she wanted to eat with us. She eagerly accepted the offer, of course, and Jim sat there bursting with pride as she relished each delicious morsel, and exclaimed that she had never seen such beautiful trout. (I ordered from the menu.)

Then there was his hunting. From the time he was able to carry a gun, he was out in the woods. He soon became a top notch marksman, because whatever he did, he demanded perfection or near perfection of himself (and expected the same from others). He was not above bragging about his skill. As his good friend, Paula, used to say with a great deal of sarcasm in her voice, "Jim is so humble!" His determination to become a great marksman stood him in good stead when he was in the Army, because he got numerous medals for his marksmanship with a variety of guns and even earned a weekend pass for being the top marksman in his—whatever it was called—company? battalion?

Partridge, ducks, geese, deer, pheasants, sharp-tailed grouse

— nothing was safe from him. If he saw them, he got them! His love of hunting was almost an obsession. During duck season, he and one of his hunting buddies would get up long before dawn to get to the potholes before the flights started. They did this day after day during duck season. During partridge and sharp-tail season, he would exhibit remarkable self-control, waiting until almost four o'clock in the afternoon to take off work and drive out to one of his favorite spots, returning just at dark—always successful. We never expected to see our husband and father on weekends during any hunting or fishing season.

It was inevitable—the sports magazines, again, plus conversations with numerous other hunters. These hunters just seem to gravitate to one other. Duck hunting, Jim learned, was great in Canada; the sky was absolutely black with ducks and geese during the migrations. The only decent thing to do was to check out all these fantastic success stories, so several of the fellows excitedly left on a week's adventure. They hired a guide, slept in a tent, were cold, wet and miserable— and had the most wonderful time of their lives! It was such a great trip, they made it an annual event for a number of years. It would have been scandalous not to take advantage of such an opportunity. No man in his right mind would ignore such gifts from God!

The pattern continued and his hunting areas extended until he, in his opinion, reached the ultimate in goose hunting—Hudson Bay. What a trip! Years later, he remembered every detail, including the fact that the weather was so terrible, planes should not have been flying!

Jim's prowess as a deer hunter was already legend before he was thirty years old. A group of fellows had built a hunting shack, accessible only by water—or ice. Jim hunted relentlessly, out early every morning and the last one to return to the shack at night. Of course, he was always successful. Before he left for the shack each year, Pat would admonish him, "Daddy, don't shoot a Mama deer, and don't shoot a baby deer." In those days, any deer was fair game. When he got back home at the end of the season, Pat had to see Jim's deer. All of the deer were hung in a warehouse in back of Olson's Store, so when he took Pat over to see his deer, he always pointed out one of the bucks, which often was what he had shot, of course. It was no secret that the fellows in his shack, "filled up" every year, and it also was no secret that part of their success in each one's getting a deer was due to Jim's cunning and expertise at deer hunting. He could honestly tell the fellows where they would be most likely to spot a deer, and if they failed to get their deer, he would eagerly "assist" them. An extremely competitive man!

Jim could not always remember dates of birthdays or anniversaries, but of the thousands and thousands of fishing and hunting trips he took, he could remember exactly whom he was with, and, more often than not, how many fish or game they got!

You will, on occasion, hear more about my remarkable husband, who truly lived life to the very, very fullest.

TITUS 2:2—*That the aged men be sober-minded, grave, temperate, sound in faith, in love, in patience.*

8

Chapter 2

It was yesterday. Long, blonde curls bouncing merrily, blue eyes sparkling, she and her mother left home. Her new patent leather shoes shone as she danced along, her tiny fingers confidently grasping her mother's hand. With the other hand, she proudly smoothed her brand new dress.

As they neared the building, her steps slowed. She hesitantly entered and the smile began to fade. They entered a room and the fingers tightened in fear. Looking up, her eyes brimming with tears, she cried, "Please don't leave me!" "Oh, please don't cry," whispered her mother, her own eyes glistening suspiciously. Tenderly releasing the clutching fingers, the mother freed her hand and soon departed, with a final glance at her helpless little girl.

Friday, the scene will be repeated, and the phrases will be the same. "Oh, please don't leave me!" again will be the desperate cry. Two hands will be clasped in a comforting grasp. Only the roles will be reversed. It will be the mother who silently expresses the futile plea, her hand reaching to her husband's for reassurance. It will be her blue eyes from which the tears fall. And now, it will be the daughter's turn—"Oh, please don't cry," she will plead.

The little patent leather shoes will be replaced by high heels. The crisp fluffy dress will now be a long, full gown. On that beautiful blonde head will rest a tasseled graduation cap.

And, yes, there was a lapse of time between the two scenes. It wasn't yesterday at all that the first incident was recorded in the lives of the family. It was almost fourteen years ago. In that time, the angelic smile was replaced at times with a frown. The shining eyes had filled with tears on many an occasion. There were hurts along the way that even parents could not prevent—or "make go away."

"Where has the time gone?" we all ask. In what seemed like only a few short weeks, how was that innocent, trusting little girl transformed into this confident, poised young lady? "We wouldn't want it any other way," we say—but really, we would. We would. We would like her back as a little girl again. "That's life, children grow up," and we watch their progress with pride, sharing each achievement and lending support and comfort during the growing process. We strive with them, urging them on to this day. And then the day arrives, and somehow, in a way, we really do not want it to happen at all!

High school graduation is a happy occasion, I guess. Parents and relatives view the proceedings with pride and love. It is one of the most important milestones in the life of every child, and all parents are thrilled to have their child attain this plateau.

"This is only the beginning," is another popular phrase at this time. True. However, whether we like it or not—and, again, we wouldn't have it any other way—this also marks the beginning of some sort of a new independence for our children. They still need our love, support and comfort, but gradually their needs for us diminish. And that is as it should be. But maybe that is why high school graduation most often finds a vein of sadness overshadowing our happiness and pride.

PHILIPPIANS 2:18—*For the same cause also do ye joy, and rejoice with me.*

Chapter 3

It is getting better now, but an air of hostility hovered over our friendly little Lake Vermilion bay for a couple of weeks. Our smiles were forced and our waves of greeting were limp and cool, little lifeless gestures. It all started when Gwenn Lilya called one morning. "Guess what we have at our place? Seven goldeneyes just left our duck box and four baby mallards, with their mother and father are swimming out in front." "My baby mallards," I shrieked, but before I could even completely establish ownership, Gwenn said firmly, "They are NOT your mallards. They are OUR mallards! That is why I am calling you. So you don't start claiming every duck in the bay again." Nonplussed by her forcefulness and greed, I backed down. She was on her way to Zup's to get cracked corn for HER—did I get that?— HER ducks!

Then, very soon JoAnne Connell called me, gloating, "Guess what we have over here?" "Well, if it is baby ducks," I said very nicely and very sweetly, without a trace of "sour grapes," "they don't belong to you. They are Gwenn's. She already called me." JoAnne contradicted, "No! They are our ducks. We watched them emerge from the nest right on our property! I am going to tell Gwenn."

To attempt to establish my rightful ownership was futile. My two neighbors did not even offer to "share." I have no idea what methods they used to contain my ducklings on their shoreline, but we did not even see the tiny balls of fluff at our place.

Anyone else would have been resentful and would have pouted. I was just magnanimously quiet. Can I help it if my head was turned the other way when they waved? They could have greeted me in a tone above a whisper. Can I help it if I did not hear them?

I was all set to forgive and forget, anyway, but in about a week we were blessed with a mother whistler and over twenty-five ducklings! She must have adopted an additional family, because all the male "duck experts" who stopped in for coffee maintained that she could not have a family that large. None of the men had ever heard of such a large brood. In fact, they had to actually see the bobbing little mass before they believed it. If I were vindictive, I would have hoped the mother whistler had ducknapped Gwenn's ducks—but I am not like that. (It would be a neat twist, though, would it not?) The whistlers were non-traditionalists in other ways, too. Newborn whistlers, the duck experts advised me, drop from the duck box and leave the area. They never return. This family stayed around for at least ten days. A couple of families of MY mallard babies also made their appearance during the next day or two.

Peace, love, warmth, friendliness and tranquility have returned to our little bay. Our smiles are genuine, our waves of greeting are sincere. It has NOTHING to do with the fact that each of us now has our own families of ducks. We are just that way—kind, sharing, wonderful people.

MARK 13:26 AND 27—*Then all mankind will see me, the Messiah, coming in the clouds with great power and glory. And I will send out the angels to gather together my chosen ones from all over the world—from the farthest bounds of earth and heaven.*

Chapter 4

Men do not like to be wrong. Of course, my brothers and my husband will maintain that men are never REALLY wrong—but will admit that sometime (on rare occasions) men are not quite as right as they usually are. When men are just a teensy bit not right, they are not too chagrined if the other faction in the discussion is a male. What men just hate is when the other person in the controversy (no longer a discussion at this point) is a female. The low point in their lives is for a female to be slightly more right on subjects which are reserved and clearly designated as strictly male turf—where women should not even be treading!

I was at a family get-together on the Sunday evening when the Vikings had won their third game of the season and was discussing the victory with my nephew, who had been a football star in high school and college and who was an assistant coach of the Golden Eagles for several years. "Yes, but wait until next week when they meet the Packers. That will put an end to the Vikings' winning streak," he said dolefully. "Not to worry," I chortled, "we are going to win! After all, we both have 3–0 records."

Now, my nephew is far too easygoing and far too kind to argue with an old aunt, who did not even know what she was talking about. "Do you really think we could win?" he smiled, "I wish you were right, but I don't think we have a chance." He had lost interest in the conversation, thinking, I am sure, that he could talk more intelligently to his five-year-old daughter. Before he walked away I got in a final statement about the Vikings' victory over the Packers the next Sunday.

A couple of minutes later, my brother crossed the room and took me aside. "Did I hear you tell John that the Vikings were going to take the Packers?" he asked. "They are," I predicted adamantly. "Phil, please don't go around saying that. I wish the Vikings would win, but they don't stand a chance. Don't keep making that statement. You embarrass not only yourself, but the whole family." To ease the sting of his statement, he patted my shoulder and said jovially, "And when did you become such an expert on football, anyway?" "What's to know?" I questioned, authoritatively "you get the ball, work it past the goalie and make a basket—simple!" Before returning to his other guests, he repeated his admonition about my keeping my mouth shut about the outcome of next Sunday's game, and I answered to his retreating back, "But we could win," however, with not quite as much conviction as my previous predictions.

When I got home, I repeated the conversations with my nephew and my brother to Jim, who had not been feeling well enough to go to the party. (I might have slanted the account just a little, to put myself in a better light.) "You didn't say that! My gosh, your brother was right. You made a fool of yourself," Jim sputtered. Husbands do not have to be as tactful as brothers, you see. Men take everything so personally. Instead of disgracing just myself, he seemed to feel that he, too, had suffered embarrassment. (What is with these men?) After having lived with me all these years, during which he had worked diligently to make me "football literate," I had shamed him beyond measure. He had been a football star in high school, and he frequently tried to teach me the finer points of the game. He went on and on about my lack of knowledge of football and about women making statements on subjects about which they know absolutely nothing. "The Vikings won't even know they are in the game," he kept repeating until I really got irritated. By that time, I was a little less sure of a Vikings' victory, but I was too proud to admit it. My confidence returned during the week, however, although it certainly was not buoyed up by most forecasts of the outcome of the game. I stubbornly refused to back down.

By Sunday, everyone was all hyped up and on the verge of an anxiety attack as the noon kick-off approached. I will have to admit—Rich, please do not read this—that in church Sunday morning when the minister asked the congregation to pray for our country and our leaders, I prayed for the Vikings. Our country and leaders would have to wait until the following Sunday for my prayers.

I was not home to watch the game, and to be honest, I am sure I probably would not have sat and watched the entire action—but I would have checked on the score frequently. I left home at the end of the first quarter when the game was tied at seven. By the time a friend and I (oh, and Bucky) had reached Ely, we learned that the Vikings were ahead. I was ecstatic! We got the scores from time to time during the afternoon, and when the Vikings fell behind, I consoled myself with the thought that even if we did lose, those wonderful Vikings had put up a good fight. Then we were ahead—and then we won! I was absolutely delirious. It took all the willpower I had not to speed home at eighty miles an hour to begin gloating.

I resolved to be charitable and gracious about our victory. I would not even mention the game when I entered the house. "So the Vikings lost," Jim said as I came through the door. Well, I threw caution to the wind. I gloated. I chortled. I was obnoxious, I was arrogant, I was disgusting, I was impossible—and I loved every minute of it. "I thought if we did win, it would have been by a smaller point spread," Jim admitted. "No, no, no. That is not what you said. You said the Vikings would not even know they were in the game. That is what you said!" I argued gleefully. He could stand it no longer, and cut me short with the statement, "Your brother called. He wanted to apologize and to check with you on your predictions for the outcomes of next week's games."

I would exercise restraint. I would not call my brother and gloat. I would be merciful and kind. If he wanted to talk to me, he could call again. It took all of thirty seconds for these generous thoughts to course through my head—and then I scurried to the telephone. He laughed good-naturedly and we agreed that I was nothing short of wonderful (well, he did not exactly say that—it was more like "you made a good guess.") As we were talking, there was a loud thump somewhere in our house and Jim shouted, "What was that noise?" I excused myself a second and then came back on the line to explain to my brother the reason for the interruption. "Could it have been a big head exploding from all that ego?" he asked. "That statement sounds as if it were coming from a poor loser," I bantered. "You're right," he laughed. I floated through the house after the telephone conversation. "My moment of glory—my one moment of glory!" I trilled. "Well, you had better enjoy it," Jim said gruffly, "it won't happen again." I took Jim's advice. I enjoyed it.

I know what you are thinking. If the outcome of a football game is my one moment of glory, what kind of a humdrum life do I lead? What have I ever achieved? You can draw your own conclusions. I agree that a football game is not a major accomplishment, given my many years of futile attempts, but I am capitalizing on that Viking win. You see, not only did the Vikings win, I won! In a world of male domination, where men still most often "call the tunes," (whether we like to acknowledge it or not) I was slightly more right than A MAN—even SEVERAL MEN! It cannot get any better than that! I am NOT a feminist—really. Jim will agree. But golly, this really feels great!!

PROVERBS 27:2—*Let another man praise thee, and not thine own mouth; a stranger, and not thine own lips. (All right guys—I am sorry!)*

Chapter 5

He is so much a part of our lives, we here in the Tower-Soudan area just take him for granted. We really do not stop to realize how very few craftsmen are left in his profession. He is unique—unique not only because he is one of the last in his trade, but also unique because he is a man of firm convictions, who adamantly sticks to his ideals.

That is our William Hulkonen. Who? "Squeaky." "Well, why didn't you say so? Who knows him by the name, William Hulkonen?" There is not a man, woman or child, however, who does not know "Squeaky," our watch and timepiece repairman. "Squeaky" said that he has no idea how he got that nickname.

Willie's fame is not limited to the local area. For decades, numerous Lake Vermilion summer home owners each year have included their valuable clocks and watches in the luggage as they prepare to come "up North" for the summer. Willie's repair shop, indicated by a modest sign in his window, is one of the first stops on their list upon their arrival here. Many families would not dream of letting anyone else clean or repair their antique clocks or priceless watches. Who else has the proper appreciation of a truly beautifully crafted watch? Who else has the patience and know-how to get Great Aunt Martha's clock running properly again?

Willie is beginning his fifty-fourth year in his own watch and clock repair business. With the advent of digital clocks and watches, timepiece repairmen are as rare as the proverbial "hen's teeth." Willie explained that nowadays, people tend to throw away their clocks and watches, rather than have them repaired.

When he reached his Golden Anniversary in business several years ago, I begged Willie for an interview. He refused, although we are good friends. I have persisted for four years and each time he tactfully postponed the interview. He was always "too busy." One evening a couple of months ago, I stopped at his home, unannounced, to try to wheedle some bits of information from him. He was not too happy about it, but, to be truthful, I persisted and imposed on his friendship.

"Squeaky" was born in Tower in 1913, the son of Mr. and Mrs. Paavo Hulkonen. The family moved to Soudan in 1918 and he attended the Soudan School through the fifth grade. In 1924, he contracted osteomyelitis, which left him crippled. "A lot of people don't like the word, cripple, but that is what it is. Crippled. I'll use that word, because that is what I am," he states firmly, with no self pity.

Willie was confined to his home for three years before he entered the Gillette Hospital in St. Paul on August 1, 1927. He spent the remainder of that year and was there throughout 1928 and until Christmas, 1929, when he came home. During his hospital stay, he completed his sixth grade education. Even after his release, he had to make periodic returns to the hospital.

In 1932, he took a course in watch repair through the state rehabilitation program. The tuition, he recalls, was $135.00. That is all he got from the state. His parents had to pay the $25.00 a month for his board and room. By today's standards, that is a most insignificant amount of money. However, he reminded me, emphasizing his statement by shaking his finger (a gesture characteristic of him), that was in the height of the Depression, and $25.00 a month was a fortune. He attended the Stone School of Watchmaking in Minneapolis for eleven months, returning to Soudan in 1933.

Willie opened his own watch repair shop in Soudan, but left in 1935 to work in a jewelry store in North Dakota. He spent less than three months there. The owner of the store also was a mortician who had his mortuary on the first floor and his living quarters on the second floor. The man and his wife met Willie at the train depot and brought him to their home. The arrangement, however, was not what Willie had in mind and he returned to Soudan to reopen his own watch repair shop.

In 1961, he opened a watch repair shop in Tower. "That was the same year that Joe Mesojedec opened his hotel and restaurant in Tower," he explained. He kept his shop open in Tower (in what is now the site of the Curiosity Shoppe) until 1964, when traveling from his home in Soudan to his shop in Tower became too much of a hardship. "Everyone advised me to go back to Soudan. They all said that I would continue to have more work than I could handle," he said. They were right. (Note: The building he occupied in Tower was located adjacent to what is now the Embarrass Vermillion Federal Credit Union and was torn down a number of years ago.)

He has repaired clocks and watches for three generations for many families. He still works every day, sometimes putting in between twelve and sixteen hours a day. In addition, he does all his own housework. "My mother died in 1954, and I have been alone and keeping house ever since," he explained.

He has two sisters, Mrs. Elden (Ann) Westman of Waukegan, Illinois and Mrs. Joe (Sylvia) Bianchi of Ely.

"The old mechanical watches are going to be out," he predicts with a characteristic wave of his hand. "The new watches are the coming thing. Some sophisticated models will program birthdays and signal you on the date, will remember telephone numbers, are musical and also are adding machines. Press a button, and they tell you the time. You can't stop progress," he said ruefully, with a shake of his head.

He described quality timepieces as "pieces of art," and explained how people are duped into purchasing "imitation" watches of inferior quality, thinking they have a quality product. "The case is often beautiful, but open the case and you can tell immediately that the works are not of good quality."

For many years, Willie sold watches, watch bands, jewelry and Ronson cigarette lighters. "A small business just can't compete with big companies," he said, explaining that his wholesale prices got to be more than the retail prices in the big chain stores. He also sized rings until the price of gold make it cost prohibitive to continue.

"I remember watches that I worked on fifty years ago," he said. "They have been passed down in families and are prized possessions now. I have lots of memories," he added. He enjoys reminiscing on the early days of Soudan, on its stalwart miners and their families. "I remember most of the people—the immigrants are all gone now. I remember them and their families."

His appreciation and enjoyment of fine timepieces has been handed down to his niece, Nancy, who collects clocks and has over forty timepieces in her home near Waukegan, Illinois. She trusts nobody but Uncle William to work on them.

He stresses the value of an education and feels that everyone should learn at least one language other than his native tongue. He, himself, speaks fluent Finnish and can read Finnish as well. He attended summer schools at the Finnish Lutheran Church in 1922, 1923 and 1924 to improve his skill at reading and writing Finnish. His instructor was the late The Rev. Evert Torkko. "I still have my report cards from those classes," he advised.

When he isn't working, Willie is reading. He loves to read. "Not fiction, though," he said. He can converse knowledgeably on a wide variety of topics, and he keeps abreast of current events and news of local, national and international happenings. He watches very little television. "Just the news," he explained. He used to enjoy sports and was an avid fan, attending the University of Minnesota football games, baseball games in Chicago and the hockey games. A man of high principles, he no longer is interested in sports. "The players are too greedy," he said. "They are mercenary. They ask for millions of dollars. They have spoiled sports for many people." Nowadays, he sticks to his reading—his magazines, periodicals and newspapers.

He admits to "a little arthritis in his hands," but stated that this does not interfere with his work. "I use tweezers, anyway," he explained.

Whether he likes it or not—whether he agrees, Willie Hulkonen is one of the GREATS of Tower-Soudan. An institution in our communities.

MATTHEW 5:16—*Let your light so shine before men, that they may see your good works and glorify your Father which is in heaven.*

Chapter 6

It was a gorgeous Autumn day. Every year I mention that indescribable Autumn aroma which permeates the forest. There is no perfume, even at $200.00 an ounce, to equal that wonderful scent. The late Howard Wagoner felt it necessary to remind me every year that the odor was only that of wet, rotting leaves, but his annual statement did nothing to lessen my appreciation of that intangible aura.

The beautiful weather begged one to get out and enjoy a perfect Minnesota Autumn day, and it did not take much to entice me to leave the housework undone and go out partridge hunting with Jim. Of course, I do not hunt. I just walk along, erring with every step. This safari starts off badly from the time I leave the car and slam the door, "alerting every partridge within ten miles." Of all the millions of things at which I am inept, hunting is right up there near the top of the list. I step on brittle branches, which explode under my feet. I stumble on rocks, sending them clattering against each other. "After all these years, I would think you would know better," Jim says in that long-suffering, exasperated tone. It probably is not the time to retort, "After all these years, I would think that YOU would know better than to invite me to go hunting." The man, let's face it, is angry and carrying a gun.

I walk too rapidly, and am reminded to slow down. I measure each step, plodding along slowly. Will you look at that? A strawberry blossom this time of the year! That maple tree. It is blinding in its brilliance of color. Its contrast against the green leaves of the adjacent birch are breathtakingly beautiful. What kind of bird is that? I know that it is some exotic bird migrating South. My mind wanders and my steps have quickened. I forgot to keep my pace slow, and have to be reminded again, "like a two-year-old." Obediently, I again slow down, determined to "do better." However, my attention span is extremely limited, and I have now placed myself in a direct line of fire if Jim should see a partridge. Another reprimand. I speak too loudly, and I feel I must converse. Hunters do not talk while pursuing their prey.

I try to concentrate on my pace, but I am distracted by the thought of what would happen if Jim saw a partridge. He is an excellent shot, and if he sighted a partridge, it would be a dead bird. I harbor guilt and traitorous thoughts. Any wife worth her salt would be cheering for her husband. I really want to, but a part of me is saying, "Hide, partridge. Hunker down. Don't move."

I come up with this terrible, wrenching scenario. What if I saw a partridge and Jim was looking the other way and did not see it? What would I do? Would I call his attention to the presence of the bird? This would be a struggle. Just imagining the situation torments me. On the one hand, Jim is a hunter, and a good one. He loves to hunt, and any decent wife would do all she could to assist him. On the other hand, why not just shoot at a target? Would that not be as great a challenge? I truly cannot bear to see anything killed. I solve my dilemma by keeping my eyes focused on the ground right ahead of me, so I would have to step on a partridge before I would see it. My conscience is clear—kind of.

Of course, Jim hunts up a partridge. Of course, he gets it. Of course, I cringe and turn away. We trudge along, and I concentrate only on all the pointers I have learned—or not learned, as the case may be. Eventually, it begins to get dusk and we head back to the car. "It has been a good day, hasn't it?" Jim asks, and thinking of the perfect Minnesota Autumn day drawing to a close, and the privilege of having been outside to enjoy it, I have to agree.

ROMANS 12:2—*Do not conform any longer to the pattern of this world, but be transformed by the renewing of your mind.*

Chapter 7

I have never completely approved of the women's liberation move-ment, so please do not think that the following statement tends to lend support to such goings-on. However, (that word always seems to follow an emphatic statement, does it not?) I feel that I must take a stand on the attitude of appliance repairmen towards the helpless female owners of the appliances. The situation has reached such a stage that I feel the only sensible solution would be to limit the appli-ance repair field to females only.

For instance, if a housewife tells a male repairman that her elec-tric steam iron heats up even when the plug is not in the socket, the man regards her with a supercilious air, looks down his nose at her and sneers. Repairmen have two stock statements: "That is mechani-cally impossible" and "It will cost more to get it fixed than a new one would cost you."

No matter how carefully and technically a housewife describes the symptoms of her ailing appliance, the repairman brushes her aside with a wave of his hand, regarding her as if she were one step lower in mentality than a moron. Now, in my Utopia, with all-female repair personnel, a housewife could make the absolutely logical statement that her vacuum cleaner, instead of slurping up the dust on the floor, has developed the habit of sploshing the contents of the vacuum bag out onto the carpet—and the intelligent, knowledgeable female "maintenance engineer" would nod in complete comprehension.

I am speaking with authority, having existed with ornery appliances for a half century. Only I know exactly which spot to hit to make the stubborn clothes washer open its lid. I do not need a repairman to tell me that a flashlight in a strategic spot on the dryer is by far the easier way to see inside the drum, once the inside light has decided that it is going to show me who is boss.

When the washer develops a sudden allergy to hot water, I simply outwit it, pretend that I do not even notice its latest campaign in its constant war against me, and I rush to the store for cold-water soap. It stands to reason (and it always works) that once the washer realizes it cannot get the best of me, it will finally give in and begin to take in hot water again.

Just try to explain these things to a repairman. He spouts off about wires, bearings, polarity, condensers, coils, intake, spark plugs and a lot of other terms, just designed to try to confuse a housewife. Now, you housewives, realizing that this is just a gimmick to throw you, need no longer be intimidated by the flow of meaningless terminology.

One thing that I must admit. It is difficult for an outsider, not acquainted with appliances, to immediately grasp the personality of each ailing piece of equipment. This does interfere with a diagnosis.

For instance, my washer is a rebel, a non-conformist—and has a mean streak! Even a repairman is awed by the behavior of this machine. All the washer has to hear is that such-and-such an action is "mechanically impossible," and he (notice the gender—that is a clue!!) immediately proceeds to undertake the impossible. After many long years of experience, during which the repairman practically lived at our home and became so much a part of the family that our daughter thought he was a relative, the "maintenance specialist" began to understand my washer. I realized this fact one day when he called me into another room, glanced surreptitiously over his shoulder at the washer and just mouthed the well-known phrase, "It is mechanically impossible."

Our toaster is of an entirely different temperament. It is happy-go-lucky and good-natured—but carefree. "So the bread is toasted on only one side," it grins from its double slots. "It's no big tragedy, is it?" There is more to life than the color of the morning toast—and this is a lesson our toaster taught us well. Set the dial on "light" and on mornings when the toaster is in a capricious mood, the bread pops up burned. Or, to add variety and suspense, there are mornings when the bread does not pop up at all!

The vacuum cleaner, on the other hand, is of a quiet, stoic nature. Hardworking, patient and non-complaining, its only fault is that it smells funny. No—really, it does. The repairman looks at me quizzically when I explain this ailment to him and ask him to at least look at it—one more time! He takes it to his shop, brings it back in a week—giving me enough time, so he thinks, to forget about the whole thing. Same old problem, compounded now by the fact that the neighbor's vacuum which I borrowed during the absence of my own, was a living testimonial for the effectiveness of a deodorant. It did not have an odor at all. I am now handling the problem myself by spraying the vacuum bag weekly with my very best cologne. It does not completely eliminate the vacuum's smell, but it does make it much more tolerable.

My electric steam iron is of a very complicated nature. I would diagnose it as having a split personality. It has suffered some abuse (I have dropped it on the floor several times) which probably tends to make it feel unwanted, and certainly must have left some emotional scars. However, one would think that the tender loving care which is lavished on it in between falls would assure it of its valued position in the family.

I will be the first to admit that the iron (and the ironing) suffer from neglect for varying periods of time, but the concentrated attention I devote to this appliance when the ironing has overflowed from all four baskets, and every other available container is piled high with unironed clothes, should more than make up for a little lack of attention once in a while. Not so. Even I, after long association with the iron, cannot always predict its actions or analyze its moods. Is it calm and tranquil today—or is it brooding? It performs well for hours on end. Then, just as I put the final touches on a mile-long white linen tablecloth, it throws a temper tantrum, spewing rust-colored water all over the freshly ironed cloth! "Gotcha," it smirks. In frustration, I snarl, "You can be replaced, you know," realizing even before the last word is uttered that I am probably contributing further to the emotional problems of the iron.

The refrigerator, on the other hand, is one appliance we do not criticize. It has been with us too many years and is too much a part of the family. Just as with people, one has to overlook faults in such a dear friend. It will not keep the ice cream in a solid state, but freezes the milk, and the way that the frost builds up on the coils is cause for alarm. However, it is loyal and faithful, and just the thought of parting with it would break my heart. So, when a member of the family suggests replacing this appliance, I loudly proclaim its merits, and the refrigerator, basking in my praise, continues to perform as well as it ever did.

Men take ailments of appliances too lightly—or else, erroneously try to find a mechanical or scientific solution to the problem. Scoff if you wish—but I can tell you of an instance (and I have witnesses!) when, after my husband had tried to start our stubborn car for at least fifteen minutes, I happened to go outside, immediately took stock of the situation, and gave the troublesome vehicle a good, hard, swift, I-mean-business kick in the bumper—and it started before my foot was even back on the ground!! (I never did get along with that car, and I could just sense its animosity whenever I drove it.) I could write a book about the conflicts between that automobile and me. Nevertheless, it seemed a hollow victory and a cowardly way out of an impossible situation when my husband finally traded that vehicle in on a new one.

JOHN 20:29—*Jesus saith unto him, Thomas, because thou hast seen me, thou hast believed: blessed are they that have not seen, and yet have believed.*

Chapter 8

So many people mentioned Mother's smile, describing it as warm, gentle, angelic, radiant. It was all of that and more. Few realized what that beautiful smile often masked—heartache, heartbreak, sorrow, worry, disappointment. Yet Mother faced the world with courage and compassion, always reaching out to comfort others, to pray diligently for others, to cheer up those who were depressed. She was a cheerful, smiling lady, who was never depressed or sad for very long. During her lifetime, she lost three beloved sons, and while others in the family questioned the unfairness of their deaths, Mother, her heart breaking, would declare, "A loving God knows best."

As her granddaughter, Shannon, noted at Mother's funeral, "Grandma was the heart and center of our family." What a perfect description. Mother's thoughts constantly centered around us, whether we were in California, Utah, right here at home or Viet Nam. She was the focal point in our lives, always praying for us, worrying about us. We sat by her bedside a number of times during the past couple of years during medical crises. Critically ill, she would reach out to hold our hand and ask how we were. She had to be assured that her children were all right.

Mother viewed her loved ones—her children, their spouses, their children and grandchildren and their spouses—through her distorted "mother's vision." We were beautiful, we were handsome, we were wonderful, we were clever, we were witty, we were hard-working (the latter was very important to Mother). I do not think that she openly expressed these views to her friends, but she made certain that we knew how she felt. I could have been dressed in a torn, ragged gunnysack, with one shoe, stockings falling down around my ankles, smudges on my face, my hair hanging in dirty, greasy chunks, and Mother would have looked at me and found me beautiful. Not that she did not see our faults and our shortcomings, but her overwhelming love for us blocked out everything else. We disappointed her, we worried her, we hurt her, but her love never wavered. Someone asked my sister if Mother ever raised her voice to us and Priscilla answered, "She didn't have to. She just looked."

Mother prayed for us constantly, but she did not confine her prayers to her family. A missionary in Africa, a friend burdened with worry, a doctor in Duluth with a personal problem, a Tower-Soudan person in the hospital, a friend struggling with a marriage, someone facing a medical crisis. Mother talked to God about everyone she knew whom she felt should be called to God's attention. Not to make light of her devotion, but in all sincerity, we often said that "if Mom is praying for you, you have all your bases covered."

Mother adored her son-in-law who lived next door to her. She would see Mick out working in the yard and, despite his vigorous protests, would join him with her rake or shovel. They were great pals, and she would work with him, thoroughly enjoying the raking or shoveling until he suggested that they stop for a snack. Mom would hurry inside and they would chat over lemonade or hot chocolate—and cookies, of course. When Mother reached her late eighties, we decided that shoveling was a little dangerous for her and demanded that she wait for Mick to come and shovel her sidewalk. It was an exercise in frustration, because someone would inform us that Mother was out shoveling, and we would confront her with the news, only to be faced with some limp excuse about why she HAD to "just clear a path." We finally won the battle when we took her shovel away. Tough love, but it was either that or have her slip and fall and break a bone. Her independence was vital to her.

The staff at the nursing home truly loved her. She greeted them with that special smile, she joked with them, she was concerned about them and with true caring would listen to their problems. They found her so amusing. "She is the only resident we have ever had who thanked us for her insulin injections," they would chuckle. And Mother did. "Thank you," she would say, her hand resting lovingly on their arm every time she received her injection, "thank you." When the Life Flight helicopter staff was preparing her for a flight to a Duluth hospital some time ago, one of the helicopter people came out of the emergency room, laughing, "She is thanking us and thanking us, and we haven't done anything!" Mother was so appreciative for every small act of kindness or favor from family or friends. She spent her lifetime adamantly determined "not to be a burden to anyone."

As the helicopter crew was getting her ready for the flight, one of them said, "This will be your first helicopter ride, won't it?" No, Mother responded, she had flown in a helicopter before. She loved airplanes, and when they were still being powered by rubber bands, Mother was flying in them. She enjoyed traveling and found airliners exciting. While my sister and I were much more timorous about air travel, Mother relished every minute of it.

She was a contradiction. Gentle, quiet, sincere, prim, proper on the one hand, she was daring, adventurous and fearless on the other. She loved life. A granddaughter's favorite story is of stopping with her husband to show off their new motorcycles to Gram and to see if she wanted to go for a ride. Gram was doing the "grandmotherly thing," baking cookies, not surprising, since she baked constantly—always for others. She was bitterly disappointed to be in the middle of baking when she could have gone for a motorcycle ride, so it was suggested that the granddaughter stay and finish the baking. "Great idea!" crowed Gram, as she donned the helmet and hurried out the door.

She was such a good sport, always cheerfully going along with whatever we wanted to do, never complaining, always appearing to enjoy herself. While I grumbled at inconveniences or forced changes in plans, Mother always looked on the bright side and tried to convince me to do the same. We always joked about the question never being IF Mother wanted to accompany us to Virginia or wherever. "It is never IF, only WHEN." I would call her—"Mom, I'm going to Virginia." "How soon?" she would ask. "Do I have time to change clothes?" If the car was going, Mom was happy to be in it.

For many, many years, she baked cookies for her family every single week. They were wonderful, absolutely the best, and our friends would eagerly anticipate what kind Gram was making that week. She never, ever, not even once, handed us the cookie tin without saying, "I don't know if they are any good. I hope they are all right. Let me know." It got so we would laughingly say, "They probably are terrible, Mom, but we will take them off your hands." Her rye bread, pasties, saffron buns and pies will never be equaled. For her friends, there was always a loaf of cherry nut bread to let them know they were in her thoughts and prayers.

She loved young people, and her grandchildren and their friends often made Mother's home their headquarters, playing piano, singing, roughhousing. And Mother was right there, eyes sparkling, pushing the cookies, making tea, hot chocolate and lemonade, listening to their problems, consoling, comforting, enjoying the music, because she loved music. They all adored her, and she was in her glory, surrounded by the young people.

For years, Mother spent countless hours sitting at her window, creating beautiful pieces of handwork for each of her children and grandchildren. What treasures that handwork has become for each of us. She would wave and smile to those who passed by on the sidewalk, and they always looked for her in that window. Mother always "wanted to be busy." She could not bear to be inactive. "I have to be doing something," she would fuss, and the closest she would come to impatience is when she had nothing to do.

Many of the nursing home staff, as well as some of our friends, mentioned in recent months that Mother seemed to be "hanging on," for her family. She, herself, was ready to go to be with her Lord. "I am so, so tired," she would sigh. The thought of her leaving us alone here on earth was impossible, and we would selfishly encourage her to eat a little more, drink a little more, do her exercises, take her medicine—try harder to get well.

Finally, after ninety-seven years (many of them tough years) she went to her reward. She was a saint. As her grandson, Michael, tearfully stated at her funeral, "Gram wasn't perfect. She made mistakes," but she was the closest thing to perfection there will ever be on this earth! She left a void which never can be filled.

PROVERBS 32:28—*Her children rise up, and call her blessed; her husband also, and he praiseth her.*

Chapter 9

This is a true story about a young couple and their dream. The story begins about twelve years ago when the girl was in college. Many of her college classmates, with much more affluent parents, spent their summers in Europe. This young lady spent her summers working to earn money to help to pay for some of her college expenses. But she began to dream of a trip to Ireland. Her dream was such a fragile thing, it seemed that just repeating it aloud would destroy it, and she harbored it within herself, confiding in no one. However, she began to put aside small sums of money in hopes that the trip would some day become a reality.

Then she met a young man, they were eventually married, and he began to share her dream.

Now, not many dreams can become realities without a great deal of effort on the part of the dreamers, and so it was with this young couple. They continued to systematically save money, with visions of the Emerald Isle in mind. It is never easy for a young couple setting up housekeeping, but this couple seemed to encounter more problems than many newlyweds. Illnesses, hospital expenses, periods of unemployment, the husband's return to college to complete his education—and, of course, the usual house payments, car payments, breakdowns of appliances, repairs and remodeling of their home, etc.

They continued to put aside money for the trip to Ireland, never completely losing sight of their goal. Many times the funds they had saved for the trip should have been spent for college expenses, hospital bills, clinic bills, etc. A more practical couple would have "dug into that sock" in numerous emergencies. When they did "borrow" from the fund, they conscientiously "repaid" the money. Each dollar that went into the "dream fund" was a sacrifice, but they kept doggedly adding small sums whenever possible.

One of the tests came when another couple, very close friends, began to make plans for a trip to Hawaii. It was tempting to use their savings to accompany the pair, but their goal was a trip to Ireland, and they stayed home, later listening to the travelers' glowing accounts of Hawaii.

They kept their objective a secret, sharing it with no one until it was time to make their announcement. And what better time to divulge their dream than St. Patrick's Day? They met with the young lady's parents and, starry-eyed, blurted out their plans. A trip to Ireland! A dream come true! The stunned parents could not believe what they were hearing. A dream of which they were totally unaware for so many years? It took them some time to comprehend. The young couple was patient, briefly relating the twelve long years of scrimping and saving for the attainment of their goal. Now, it was time for that trip to Ireland. Enough money had been saved for the two tickets and for the other expenses of the trip for THE YOUNG LADY'S PARENTS!! You see, that was the dream all those years. It wasn't for the couple that the money had been saved. It was to provide a trip to Ireland for the girl's parents.

Fiction, you'll say. No, fact! And I know, because we are the parents. Of course, we argued. We adamantly refused their generous offer. Knowing how much they both needed a vacation themselves, we insisted that the money be used for a trip to Ireland for themselves. We stood firm—but they brushed aside our arguments. The money, they said, would be used for no other purpose. We suggested possible uses they had for the funds—they wouldn't even listen.

And so, a couple's dream is going to come true. We will be making a trip to Ireland this year, God willing. Each dollar was saved with love and sacrifice, and it just doesn't seem right for us to accept such a gift, but our protests fall on deaf ears. A trip to Ireland has long been a dream of ours, but all we have ever done is dream—it took our daughter and her husband (our son) to make a dream come true.

PSALM 136:1—*O give thanks unto the Lord; for he is good; for his mercy endureth forever.*

Chapter 10

"Your car is filthy," Jim said the other day. Have you wives ever thought about it? While it is not written in textbooks, there is definitely what I will call "the language of marriage." The statements made by husbands do not always mean what one thinks the words would indicate.

Jim's statement did not endow ownership, just responsibility. Now, let me make this perfectly clear. I am generalizing. I am not talking about Jim, who has issued some very unpleasant, ominous threats about what will happen if I keep writing about him. So—again—let me emphasize that this is not about anyone in particular. What is the phrase? Any similarity to any living person is entirely coincidental?

I digress. "Your son's diaper needs changing." "Your daughter is fussy because she wants her bottle." "Your television screen is so dusty I can write my name on it." "Your fire needs more wood." "The oil should be changed on your car." "Your dog wants to go out." "Your checkbook needs balancing." To you young, naïve brides, your husband, making such statements, rest assured, is not relinquishing ownership of anything at all. He is bestowing responsibility—nothing more!

However, it is extremely complex. Sometimes, he really does mean your, and it is like a warranty deed. No doubt about it, you own it—whatever it is! An example: "I lost your silver Rapala when I was out fishing today." The man is incredible! Two silver Rapalas in the tackle box. Both the same size. Both—not floaters—sinkers?? Whatever. The husband unerringly knows it is your Rapala he lost. "You had better mark it on your shopping list so you can get another one," he reminds you thoughtfully.

"You are out of Coke." "You need more potato chips." "You are out of Snicker Bars." Do you ever wonder why you do not seem to notice the lack of these commodities in the cupboard when it is you who do not have them? I guess you wives out there really should be grateful you have someone who helps out with the grocery list. (As I pointed out, I am not involved in this.)

Back to the opening sentence of this column: The only time in my life that I took the car to a self-service car wash was years ago when I was traveling in Canada—sans husband. The equipment was antiquated, by today's standards. But I did what I considered a very good job of washing the car. My mother and my niece, who accompanied me on the short trip, were proud of me.

Jim's statement about the filthy condition of the car got me thinking about venturing into what has been alluded to (at least in our home) as strictly male territory. I would take the car to The Car Wash—all by myself! I took Bucky along as technical advisor. I needed support to enter this great unknown, and Bucky is an amiable partner, never ruffled by little glitches.

I got $3.00 in quarters from Julie at Zup's. "The laundry or the car wash?" Julie laughed. As if I were setting out on a dangerous adventure, I informed her I was headed for the car wash, and off I sped. Drove up—read the instructions for opening the door. Already I am intimidated. I push the right button, the door opens! "Piece of cake," as by brother used to say. I drive in—read the instructions for closing the door. I accomplish this remarkably well, and I am well on my way to washing the car. I read the instructions about using the brush. I read them again to firmly implant them in my mind. Crossing over to the other side, I read the instructions about actually getting this operation underway. This is a little more complicated. I read them again, decide against the wax, read them once more—and insert my $1.50. I rush over to the wand, waiting in anticipation. Nothing happens. I just lost $1.50! I have only $1.50 left. Panic sets in. Can I complete this entire operation for just $1.50 worth of time? I run back to the coin machine, only to find that it has rejected one of my quarters. I insert the quarter again, and am rewarded by a stream of water gushing from the wand.

I do not feel that it is necessary to go into the mistakes I made. All it takes is common sense, but I am so easily intimidated by anything new, no matter how simple the procedure, that common sense completely eludes me. For instance, I do not think that the management intended for me to use the brush with one hand while juggling the wand with the other. It was clumsy! Other glitches are too embarrassing to mention.

Bucky and I got that car washed. It was not a first-class job, but my car looked quite nice as I pushed the right button to open the door, drove out, and miraculously pushed the proper button which closed the door. At least, I have the opening and closing of the doors perfected. I guess it was not such a great wash job, however. Jim did not even notice that the car looked sparkling clean—well, cleaner, anyway.

Could I give just one little tip to you wives who might want to venture into a car wash? A forceful stream of water suddenly directed at the side mirror of a vehicle will automatically (I think it is a rule of physics or something) and with equal force, reverse direction completely—I think it would be 180°—and we know what is located at the 180° mark, don't we?

GALATIANS 5:22–23—*The fruit of the spirit is love, joy, peace, patience, kindness, goodness, faithfulness, gentleness and self-control.*

Chapter 11

I worked late last Wednesday night, so it was dark when I got home. I slept in on Thursday morning, and when I finally awakened, I stumbled downstairs, my eyes barely open. The sight that confronted me popped my eyes open and shocked me awake. In our front yard was a beautiful, exquisite, gorgeous miniature log cabin. It was on the pole which had held the pathetic, battered, splintered bird feeder, which also had been beautiful in its day.

It is the prettiest, most elaborate feeder I have ever seen. It is large, with side windows and shutters, a front picture window and shutters and a door, a chimney and a tree at each end of the front "yard." The house itself is a natural wood color, while the trim is a pretty green.

I called our neighbors, and Dolores answered. She hesitated when I asked if Ron had happened to be down at our place. ("Down" because their home is on a towering cliff-edged hill, while ours is in a lowland.) Dolores finally admitted that it was Ron who had placed the bird feeder. He had made it from small logs and knowing that I usually work late on Wednesday, he had waited until then to install it on the pole.

Ron makes gorgeous furniture, which puts any "store furniture" to shame. He is a craftsman. When I expressed my appreciation for his gift, he said that he had made a number of the bird feeders for family members and had an extra one in his workshop.

That couple gives a whole new meaning to the word, "neighbors." Jim and I have always counted them as one of our blessings, believe me! They are absolutely perfect neighbors.

ROMANS 3:23—*For all have sinned, and come short of the glory of God.*

Chapter 12

I would estimate that of the more than eleven hundred people who
plan to attend the All-Class Reunion this summer, one thousand
of us are trying to lose weight. I'm not sure what we are attempting to
prove, unless it is that we have exclusive rights to the mythical Foun-
tain of Eternal Youth.

I have never seen so many running, jogging, bicycling, walking,
starving people in my life! We are all going around with sunken cheeks
and that emaciated look, drooling over the dog's food, we're so hungry.

Is it a law of physics which states that "Matter can neither be created nor destroyed"? Just ponder this a minute. I would estimate
from conversations with many of the alumni that there are one thousand of us hoping to lose an average of fifteen pounds each. (Some
have even set the unattainable goal of thirty pounds—ridiculous!!)
That is fifteen thousand pounds—seven and a half tons of fat! Where
does it go? I can't believe it is all converted into energy.

Now, I know from personal experience that not everyone will
achieve his or her goal. Every time I lose a half a pound, I reward
myself with a hot fudge sundae, and gain a pound. However, I know
of some disciplined people who had set a goal of fifteen pounds and
when they reached it, they decided to go for twenty. Naturally, they
won't even have strength enough to get to the reunion, but they keep

right on a-jogging and a-starving, and tell me they are feeling great. No Way!

One would think that our classmates didn't know how old we were! Marttila Drug already has had a run on hair dye like you wouldn't believe. Apparently the word got around because when I went to pick up a bottle—not for myself, you understand!—the supply was really low, but Walt assured me that he would have a shipment in within a day, and that included in the supply would be dye in my color—gray. (Some day I'm really going to think of a good comeback to use when Walt insults me.)

PROVERBS 16:31—*White hair is a crown of glory and is seen most among the godly.*

Chapter 13

For months, as former students of the Tower-Soudan Schools have awaited the All-Class Reunion, each one has reveled in his/her special memories of school days in Tower-Soudan. Each generation, of course, has its own special memories, decidedly different from preceding or succeeding generations.

For me and my contemporaries, our introduction to education was a delightful, exciting experience, with our kindergarten teacher, Louise Kitto, making our abrupt break from the security of our homes and the loving presence of our mothers far less painful and traumatic than it otherwise would have been. We grew up in the "old days," when there were no day-care centers or pre-schools. The focal points of our young pre-school lives were our homes. Church on Sundays, playing in our yards or close neighborhoods, visiting our grandparents and other relatives. We led extremely sheltered, simple, family-oriented lives.

Then, suddenly, we were forced to broaden our horizons and enter kindergarten. It could have been a terrifying experience were it not for Miss Kitto. She became a legend in our schools, teaching at least two generations of children in most families. (Those were the years when Tower-Soudan families "stayed put." Seldom—very seldom— did a "new" family move in, and almost never did any family move out. Why would they?)

For decades, Miss Kitto continued to lend an air of excitement to every single day of her classes. She never lost her warmth, enthusiasm, zest and love of children. She had limitless vitality which never waned throughout all those years.

How many of her pupils remember: All of the class skipping awkwardly around in a circle as she played lively music on the piano, calling out encouragement and instructions? Painstakingly cutting out circles from "construction" paper, with admonitions to "stay on the line?" Making paper chains to decorate the class Christmas tree? (I can still smell that white paste and remember the disgust some of us felt when a fellow classmate would EAT the paste!) Making Halloween pumpkins from orange "construction" paper, and drawing in the faces with black crayons? Coloring pictures with crayons as Miss Kitto repeatedly instructed us to "stay within the lines!"

Miss Kitto's favorite color was red. Most of her dresses and all of her hats and coats were always red. She wore her beautiful, thick hair in a bun, but as she bustled around, flitting from pupil to pupil, tiny wisps of hair would fall around her face, and I can still see her hurriedly tucking them back, securing them with one of those huge tortoise-shell hair pins.

Every child was a "little doll," and she truly loved her pupils. Even after several decades, she could recall the thousands of students for whom she had opened the doors of knowledge and remember something unique about each one.

Our kindergarten bands might have lacked musical talent, but we more than made up for that failing with our enthusiasm. Triangles, drums, tambourines and a xylophone, to the rousing accompaniment of Miss Kitto's piano playing. Our music would have made the composers of the songs cringe, but we thought we were wonderful. Our band uniforms were truly magnificent—they really were—and for performances at programs, we wore makeup, which was not an everyday commodity in most of our homes and created more than a little excitement. One classmate, chosen as the band leader, wore a more elaborate costume and got to conduct the band, to the envy of all of us.

Both Tower and Soudan pupils had Miss Kitto as their kindergarten teacher. She taught in one school a half day and then went by school bus to the other school.

When it was necessary to mete out discipline, she did so firmly, but always added a hug. We all loved her and longed for her approval, so it was very seldom that any pupil misbehaved.

How she ever got all of us ready to return home on the bitter cold winter days, I will never know. Every child was well prepared to face the cold weather before marching out of her classroom. She checked to make sure that scarves were tied over faces (most often performing that task herself), that mittens were securely on each tiny hand and that coats, jackets, boots and snow pants (yes, heavy wool snow pants) were all buttoned and fastened securely.

Remember our school nurses—Miss Hursh and Miss Myrtle Johnson, to name two? It was not too uncommon to feign an illness to get into the nurse's office for some tender loving care, meted out in full measure.

Those of us in Soudan went on to enjoy other teachers, always under the watchful eye of our principal, Theodore Wantke, whose very position as principal made him an intimidating, imposing personage, with whom none of us wanted to reckon, believe me! Our introduction to reading and writing was under the tutelage of our first grade teacher, Miss Eleanor Congdon, a local girl who went on to marry Glenn Pearson. Then it was petite Lorraine McGillvary (who moved away and married Dan Dasovich) -- then another local girl Wilma Western (now Wilma Farrow who lives in California)— then another local girl, Margaret Driscoll, who moved away but later returned to teach in Tower-Soudan again for a number of years— and our sixth grade teacher, Miss Connelly, a strict, no-nonsense disciplinarian, who felt that by the time pupils had reached sixth grade they should have attained at least a small degree of maturity,

47

common sense and self-discipline and have an insatiable desire to learn, learn, learn.

Through many of these years, our classes were visited by Frances Vail, the music teacher, who would go from class to class, trying to teach us to sing. Remember music appreciation class, where we fidgeted as she played classical music on the phonograph? For our tests, we had to identify the musical numbers as she played the records.

Our grand operettas, "concerts" and other programs were held at the Finnish Temperance Hall, located near the corner of Jasper and First Street. Our school had no gymnasium or stage, and the Temperance Hall had a grand stage. We often wore elaborate crepe paper costumes, which were totally ineffective in protecting us against the chill of the Hall during a winter "performance."

In those days, pupils attended the school in their own community (Tower or Soudan) through eighth grade and then we all went to the Tower School for what was, at that time, four years of high school. We were freshmen when the educational structure changed—kindergarten, six years of elementary, three years of junior high school and three years of senior high school. The new Soudan School was completed while we were freshmen, and we can all remember that momentous day during the middle of our freshman year when all freshmen gathered their books and other belongings, boarded the school bus and rode to Soudan to enter the brand new school!

Initiation for freshmen was a big occasion in the high school. Each senior was assigned a freshman "subject" for a whole day. The "subject" had to wear a costume which had earlier been designated by the "master," carry the senior's books, bow whenever the two met in the halls and, in effect, do the senior's bidding all day. The "hazing" program was held during the evening, and freshmen were fearful and apprehensive all day, listening to the stories of what would befall them during the program. Some years, the freshmen had to parade down Main Street.

After sixth grade, we had numerous instructors, the turnover more frequent than usual because some of the male teachers went into the military. (It was the World War II years.) Remember: Ellen Swanson—Esther Belle Moore (now Mrs. Sulo Holm)—Melvin Norsted ("How long is a long time?")—Stella Holt—Marjorie Fulton—Kenneth Satterfield, our principal, as well as our chemistry teacher—Meryl Kubacki—Joe Brula—Evelyn Malley—Angela Mayerle—our fantastic instrumental music teachers, first Reinhold Darm, and then Charles Minelli—Miss Pierce—Marjorie Hermann—another legend, Grace Pratt, the business education teacher, who taught typing, shorthand and bookkeeping. Even students who did not take those subjects will never forget Miss Pratt, whose penuriousness must have saved the district thousands of dollars each year (probably as much as her salary). Long before the "Save Our Trees" campaign, Miss Pratt was saving every scrap of paper over an inch square. In her class, a student did not waste a thing—discarded bookkeeping forms could be utilized for notes, pencils were used until we could no longer hold them. Losing a pencil was not acceptable. Will any of us ever forget her stern admonition to "dump that gum!!" A colorful person, she also was a dedicated teacher, and students with a will to learn went on to business school after graduation, only to find that there was nothing more to learn there. She was thorough and her students truly received a business education if they "put their minds to it," as she used to say. The list goes on and on, each one making an indelible impression on our lives.

Remember some of our coaches—Melvin Norsted, Mr. Miller, Melvin "Andy" Anderson, Mike Weinzierl, J. E. Morcombe?

Remember our high school "assembly room," where all high school classes gathered each morning for roll call before classes began and at the close of each school day to be dismissed? Our principal, Kenneth C. Satterfield (who kept everyone in line by just looking at them) would read the "tardy list," the "absence list," the dreaded summonses to appear in his office, as well as all the other announcements

49

pertinent to the coming day's activities, all delivered in his command-ing, forceful voice. The more timid of us would often have preferred to attend school with a 104° fever than to approach Mr. Satterfield to request an absence slip upon our return to school. Do not ask me why we held him in such awe and fear. I do not remember a time that he was unpleasant when I had to get the required slip. Remember having to "make up" our work and have each high school teacher sign our slip to indicate that we had completed the work we missed? That was another announcement each day: "The following students must submit their completion slips before leaving school today."

The school newspaper, "The Ta-Sa-Ha" was born during our high school years. Those of us who worked on the newspaper staff will never forget the hours of typing stencils and "running them off on the mimeograph machine," then assembling the pages. The entire process was under the direction and watchful eyes of Miss Pratt, who was never satisfied with less than perfection. We also had a girls' Pep Squad, uniformed marching unit, which conducted precision (at least we thought so!) drill performances at basketball games.

Each generation has its own great memories, its own teachers, its own highlights. Each generation writes its own capsulated account of those wonderful school years in Tower-Soudan. Wonderful, wonder-ful memories.

2 CORINTHIANS 13:8—*For we can do nothing against the truth, but for the truth.*

Chapter 14

The dazzling glitter of the sunshine on the snow was deceiving. It looked like a comparatively mild winter day. In reality, however, the mercury in the thermometer was standing on tiptoe in an unsuccessful attempt to reach the zero mark. It was, my husband announced, an ideal day for going snowshoeing.

Apparently, he had been looking at the same magazine that I had. A full-page spread of this long-legged, shapely, gorgeous model on snowshoes against a background of glistening snow and blue sky. She looked vibrant, beautiful, graceful, deliriously happy to be snowshoeing—in a word, disgusting! She wore an elegant nylon ski ensemble in a flattering shade of blue as a second skin. The wind playfully caressed the ends of her long blonde hair.

With this nauseating scene in mind, I prepared for my own outdoor winter experience. (One never goes skating, skiing or hiking these days. One has an "outdoor experience.") I have forty pounds and forty years on that model, but you know the old saying: If life hands you lemons, make lemonade. I decided on a layered look, rather than a $500.00 outdoor winter experience ensemble. I donned layer after layer after layer of warm clothing, sox, boots, and mittens. I accented this ensemble with a wool tam, adjusted at a jaunty angle, a pair of sunglasses and a wool scarf my nephew had made for me. I knotted the scarf low, as I had seen the young women do.

My arms extended in an ape-like position, with all the clothing I was wearing. I clomped and staggered my way to the shed to get the snowshoes. Well, there was no way I could bend down to get them on, and my husband had to tackle that task for me.

I took a few tentative steps and decided that snowshoeing was not all that difficult, especially if one were accustomed to walking astraddle a two-foot fence. Feet must be placed far enough apart to prevent tramping down on the opposite snowshoe when taking a step. Encouraged, I set off, clumsily plodding along, panting with the effort.

My nose got cold, so I stopped to retie the scarf around my face. My tam kept slipping off, and I continued to jam it back on my head until my hair stuck out at all angles and hung down in my face. My sunglasses fogged up, the belt of my jacket became untied and trailed in the snow, further complicating my progress, the scarf kept slipping down off my face—and then my nose started to run.

You would-be snowshoers can benefit from my experience. You CANNOT fall down with snowshoes on. If you do, prepare to stay there until the snow melts in the spring. Another thing you cannot do is turn around on snowshoes—you just have to keep walking in a straight line forever and ever.

My husband, five miles ahead of me, waited with barely disguised impatience until I huffed, puffed and snorted my way to him. "Why are you all doubled up? Stand up straight," he ordered. I had not even realized that I was walking with my nose practically touching the tips of the snowshoes. It must have something to do with the center of gravity, or something, because every time I tried to obey his order and straighten up, I felt myself losing my balance.

"I think twenty miles is enough for one day, don't you?" I asked hopefully. For an answer he led me off the trail, explaining that breaking our own trail was part of the enjoyment of snowshoeing. I stared at him, thinking he had to be joking. Instead, he swung along smoothly, his tracks marring the surface of the sparkling snow.

Suddenly, horror of horrors, my foot slipped from the binding or stirrup or whatever holds feet to snowshoes (vice versa). I shouted an S.O.S. to my husband, who instructed, "Bend your knee and your ankle and slip your foot back in." What a sense of humor he has! When I flexed my ankle the snowshoe moved with it, and in spite of all my contortions, I just could not begin to maneuver my foot into the elusive piece of leather. It was inevitable—I fell! "Bring me food every day, will you?" I pleaded as he stormed back to assist me. There was just no way I could get back on my feet. I didn't know if his face was red from anger or from the exertion of trying to get my blimp-like shape back into a more or less erect position. The snowshoe and I were both too old for this—a strap had broken.

"Why don't I just take the snowshoes off?" I asked, inspired. It seems that this would not be playing the game. Both of us were gasping for breath before I was on my feet (so to speak) and the broken strap was wound around and tucked in securely.

Our next "experience" was going uphill. It seems there is no end to the excitement of this sport. The snowshoes began to behave like skis, sliding downhill with every awkward step I took. "Hang onto the bushes and pull yourself up," the recreation director commanded. I don't want to go into detail about this phase of my experience. I'll give you a hint, though—it took a mighty sturdy bush to support me, and many didn't stand the test.

Things went downhill from there—figuratively and literally. Turning around was another lesson. (One takes tiny, tiny sideways steps, and after a hundred or so, one finds oneself pointed in another direction or collapsed in a heap on the ground.)

Apparently, I was just not a "fun-type" person, and I ruin everyone else's enjoyment of an "outdoor experience." Through clenched teeth, my mate snarled, "Let's head for home." I redoubled by efforts at staying erect. There was no problem keeping a smile on my face.

Mother was right. One's face does freeze and stay like that—and I had started out smiling, all right.

The stillness was deafening as we retraced our steps, my husband in the lead just far enough so he didn't have to speak to me. Whether or not it was deliberate, I'll never know, but within sight of our home, he left the trail again and started through a swamp. Determined to be of no more bother, I followed meekly, carefully placing my foot with every single step.

This does not have a happy ending. In spite of all my concentration and effort, my foot flipped out of the harness (or whatever) again. I could be braver now. Even if my husband deserted me, I could get home alone. "I'm taking these stupid snowshoes off," I screamed in frustration. "Use your head, woman," he shouted back. "Without snowshoes, you would sink up to your waist in this swamp." He had had enough, too. I was left to struggle into the stirrup by myself. With those blasted over-sized tennis rackets finally secured to my feet well enough to get me home, I stumbled into the shed, somehow flopped down on the floor, and attempted to free myself. For something that fell off a few minutes earlier, that snowshoe held tenaciously to my foot.

Finally extricating my feet, I crawled into the house, leaving the snowshoes on the shed floor. The weaving seemed to shape into a malicious grin as I took one last backward glance at them.

Our evening was quiet and peaceful—mostly quiet. VERY QUIET!

I CORINTHIANS 12:21—*And the eye cannot say unto the hand, I have no need of thee: nor again, the head to the feet, I have no need of you.*

Chapter 15

A serious, almost apprehensive look, has replaced the perpetual mischievous twinkle in his blue eyes. He shrugs uncomfortably as he tries to adjust his broad shoulders to the contours of his unfamiliar garment. He attempts, without complete success, to affect an air of nonchalance, waiting for the strains of the processional to begin.

We watch with love and pride as we single him out of the solemn, moving procession. He had feigned annoyance and disgust at our solicitude earlier in the evening, but we noted with satisfaction that he stole a sidelong glance our way as he passed.

The graduating class is seated on the stage, and as we watch the proceedings with tear-filled eyes, we grasp desperately at memories, capsulating his eighteen years into what we incorrectly called his "childhood years," realizing that it has been a long time since he was actually a child.

Tonight he will leave the building for the last time as a student. Wasn't it only yesterday that he entered the same building for the first time? A small, wiry, blonde boy, his blue eyes solemn and questioning. His tiny shoulders shrugging uncomfortably in the confines of his brand new first-day-of-school clothes, which, his mother had admonished him frequently on the way, MUST be kept clean.

Fiercely, independent, masking his hesitancy, fears and suspicions, he sauntered along with an air of bravado, refusing the comforting assurance of his mother's hand. His steps slowed gradually as the school building loomed into sight.

The parting of mother and child was emotional, and the mother dared not indulge herself with a backward glance at her tiny son. It was she, not he, who suffered the pangs of desertion.

The years flew by. The boy grew into a young man. The slim shoulders suddenly broadened.

There were hurts, fears, frustrations and injustices along the way. While we were aware that successfully conquering each trial builds character and provides strength to face other crises in life, we sometimes could not help but succumb to the temptation to serve as a buffer between him and the world. Some hurts could not be "made better" by loving parents and there were the usual trials each boy faces as he approaches manhood.

Reminiscing again, we remember the ingenious way he had of transforming a pair of brand new trousers into rags—in less than ten minutes. Given the challenge, we knew that he could have performed this miracle at least five times a day. It was frustrating and maddening at the time; now it is a precious memory.

We watched with loving tenderness as he painfully wrestled with childhood, then teen-age, problems. We agonized over the delicate balance between being supportive and being overly protective. The doubts were not all his—the parents, too, faced indecision. When to be silent, when to question, when to offer advice, when to let him work out the problem himself. When to punish, when to withhold disciplinary measures.

His childhood perplexity at parental rules. "Don't you dare fight," he was warned, with his parents graphically outlining the punishment should he disobey. So, he stoically suffered the abuse of his classmates for a short time until his parents realized what was happening and the rules were relaxed. He immediately beat up every kid on the block, and the rules had to be amended again.

As he matured, there was an imperceptible point at which the roles became slightly reversed, and the family members found themselves going to him for assistance. Would he repair this? Would he take care of that? Could they have his help at this undertaking? What was his opinion of this? He was there to lend strength, understanding and assistance.

Now, he will be facing more important, more serious decisions, some of which could permanently change the direction of his life. In our present permissive society, there is still right and wrong, and he will be confronted with the responsibility of establishing his own moral code, based upon (we hope!) what he has been taught.

We watch him proudly join the recessional. It is time to loose the ties before they break. We dislike the description of "cutting the ties," and that we absolutely refuse to do. We will loose them, allowing for continued growth, but we will never, ever completely "let go!"

REVELATION 22:21—*The grace of our Lord Jesus Christ be with you all. Amen.*

Chapter 16

With all the tragedy and heartbreak in the world, the death of a dog doesn't seem too important, unless it is YOUR dog. Then your grief is very real. Lucky was our dog, and Tuesday of this week we watched her bravely die. Fortunately, we were spared the heartbreak which a lot of dog owners experience—the tragedy of having their pet poisoned or run over by a car. Old Lucky died of illness—an illness, incidentally, of which we had been aware for eighteen months.

There isn't a person who visited The News office—customers, salesmen, children with their mothers—who didn't know and genuinely like our Lucky. She was a truly sweet dog. Shocked mothers would expect the worst as their children pulled Lucky's ears or tail, but Lucky seemed to realize that they did not know they were hurting her, and she would patiently sigh and get up and walk away.

In her day, Lucky, a black Labrador, had fantastic hunting ability. Her only fault, if it could be called such, was her over-abundance of enthusiasm for hunting of any kind. "A born hunter" never applied to any dog more than it did to Lucky. She could smell a grouse or a partridge a block away, and a duck didn't stand a chance of escaping from her keen nose. She loved to hunt—and the mere act of taking a gun out of the closet would send her dashing excitedly underfoot; her exuberance was hard to control until she had settled herself, panting excitedly, in the car. Her ears would perk up at the very phrase, "Want to fetch 'em up, Lucky?"

Old Lucky, of course, was not without her small faults. She instinctively knew which members of the family commanded obedience—and which ones she could ignore. She longed to please at all times, and punishment never had to be more than a cross word. Before a command was barely spoken, she was carrying it out—unless it happened to be spoken by one of the family who didn't have the heart to scold her if she wouldn't obey. She really took advantage of those who were too easygoing with her.

For years, we would return home to find the door leading to the apartment standing ajar, and we would chide each other for being careless. As in all families, of course, no one was ever guilty, and we all stated emphatically each time that we had carefully shut the door. It wasn't until one day, after dear old Lucky had lost her sight, that an incident happened to explain our open door. The outside door closed as the family left the house, and Lucky (her sight gone and not realizing that one member of the family was still present to witness her act) hurried over to the apartment door, tail wagging excitedly. One blow of her experienced paw at the proper spot on the door sprung the loose-fitting catch. A nose, expertly inserted into the small opening, completed her task and she wagged her tail in pride. I can just imagine how amused she was later as she heard us scolding about the open door—while she lay smugly and innocently nearby. (I have no doubt but what she understood almost everything we said.)

She left us with many wonderful memories. Hunters will never cease to tell the story of how she once retrieved a large walleye (floundering in the shallows) while in the process of retrieving some ducks. We will never forget how she pouted dramatically when she sensed (as she always did) that she was not going to accompany us when we left the house. She had her favorite "pouting place," and as soon as the activity indicated that she was going to be left home, she made a big act of going to that spot and there she chose to lie, completely ignoring us. Our efforts at soothing her before we left were to no avail, and these were the only times that I remember that she didn't wag her tail.

She had other ways of punishing us for leaving her home, too. One was to tip over her dish of food. She knew it annoyed us, and when she was scolded, she looked up as if to say, "It serves you right."

She dearly loved attention. A well-healed paw, when brought to her attention, would suddenly become extremely painful and she would again begin to limp and pant in agony—until her sympathizer was out of sight. Having hunted with them a lot, her joy was unrestrained whenever Bob Olson or Bill Burgess or Bob Larson— or several others—visited the shop. They always showered her with attention—and she loved it.

Lucky would have been thirteen years old in May. We had her for about twelve years. We felt as every dog owner does about his dog— there never was a dog like her! We would sometimes become impatient as we searched the shop for one of our shoes or boots which she carried around incessantly—but never chewed. We were heartbroken when the veterinarian confirmed our suspicions that Lucky was losing her eyesight. Even with her sight impaired, Lucky did a pretty fair job of retrieving—until, completely blind, she would go out into the water after a duck, and sightless, swim in desperate, determined circles, unable to find her way back to shore. We tried to make things easy for her—keeping chairs and other obstacles in place. She could navigate around the shop and around the yard with no trouble, until a chair, a car parked in the yard, or another unexpected object blocked her path. She would then become confused and hesitant— but never helpless.

Yes, old Luck fought her heart illness for eighteen months— about fifteen months more than the veterinarian had anticipated. Her last months could not have been too pleasant for her—in spite of the medications which we gave her to help ease her condition. We spent many painful hours trying to bring ourselves to follow the vet's

60

suggestion to have her "put to sleep," but we could never bring our-selves to the point of actually putting our faithful, trusting dog into a car to carry out the action. Knowing Lucky, I am positive that she would knowingly have walked into the veterinarian's office to be "put to sleep," if she thought that was what we expected and wanted of her. She was that kind of a dog.

2 CORINTHIANS 5:7—*For we walk by faith, not by sight.*

Chapter 17

The way I look at it, life can go one way or the other. One can either go through life acquiring new knowledge and new skills and reaching new horizons, OR one can live one's years expanding the list of things at which one is a failure.

Not by choice, believe me, it seems that my life takes the latter direction. The longer I live, the more things I seem to be incapable of doing well. (If one has a husband, it is easier to determine the direction one's life is taking, because husbands help by pointing it out.) High on my list of failures is the use of a camera, followed by the use of a snowblower, the use of a lawnmower—and on and on.

The latest item on my list of failures is berry picking. Jim came from a family of berry pickers, who sometimes placed this task in the category of recreation by taking along a picnic lunch and having FUN! I doubt if my father would have picked berries if he were starving, and I am sure that my dear patient mother would not have considered taking her brood on such a venture, unless she tied us all to trees. After we all grew up, Mom joined her friends on berry picking excursions, and had a lot of fun pursuing this pastime, because Mother really enjoys a challenge.

The glowing accounts of my boss, Tony, regarding the abundance of blueberries and the size of the berries finally convinced me to join Jim in a berry picking venture over the weekend. (I was further persuaded by Jim's frequent repetition of the statement that SOME people—and I knew that he didn't mean Bucky—seem to conveniently "sit around" at home while other hardworking people—again, not Bucky—are out breaking their backs and dislocating and bruising their knees in a dedicated effort to provide the stay-at-home with enough berries so that SHE (get the picture?) can "pig out" on blueberry pie.)

I join Jim at the car. He is armed with a one-gallon ice cream pail. I am carrying a one-pound margarine tub. This contrast in the size of the containers does not go unnoticed, except by Bucky, who already is in the back seat of the car, happy to be going ANYWHERE, even if it is berry picking.

We reach what Jim describes as a berry patch. This is not my very first attempt at berry picking, but I remember a berry patch as a flat, wide open area. This patch harbored thick brush, trees (both upright and fallen), rocks and rock ledges. I stumbled and staggered to the first blueberry bush.

Now, I have to explain, Jim was a Sergeant in the Army. He was in cryptography, but it must have been before he launched into that career that he sometimes led the men in formations on the parade grounds. (I didn't know Jim during that time, and I am sure that there have been times when he wishes the situation had remained that way.) Anyway, when Jim told those men to "about face," they about faced. When he told them to "halt," they halted. When he ordered, "Hut," believe me, they hutted.

So Jim assumes that is the way life is. He gives an order, and it is immediately obeyed. He took on the status of a General in the berry patch, since he was the top ranking officer. "Pick over here," he would order, and then become impatient if I dallied along the way. "Don't waste time there," he would command. Even from a distance I could hear the berries plunking into his pail at a rapid staccato rate, while I languidly plucked a berry here and there. "There's a beautiful patch here that I'll save for you," he would offer generously, "move over here." It was not even necessary for him to add, "NOW!"

The terrain was dangerous, practically life threatening. Between each berry, I would studiously check myself for the presence of a wood tick, meanwhile chasing away mosquitoes and gnats. Not only is the grass greener somewhere else, but the berries also are bluer and bigger—at least, that is what I thought.

"Look," Jim would point out. "You said you picked this patch. Look at all the berries here!" he would exclaim. "I think we should save some for the bears and the birds," I would answer lamely.

It started to rain, and Jim suggested that, perhaps, I would rather go back to the car and wait for him. Nothing doing. I was going to suffer through this.

Need I go on? I heroically emerged from that jungle with my margarine tub full, congratulating myself every step of the way. I was great at picking berries! Then I saw Jim's big gallon pail—not really full, but its contents were, indeed, impressive! He tried so hard to be magnanimous about the situation, even congratulating me on my efforts. However, I am SURE that I saw a very smug look on his face as he glanced from one container to the other. (He SWEARS I misinterpreted his expression.) His foray into the berry patch the following day was by himself, without even an invitation to me to accompany him.

PROVERBS 13:23—*Much food is in the tillage of the poor; but there is that is destroyed for want of judgment.*

Chapter 18

How many of you remember the annual Sunday School Christmas programs of "the old days?"—like sixty or seventy years ago? The youngsters of today have far more poise and sophistication than we did, and they seem to take their participation in the program in stride—or maybe it just seems that way, now that we are spectators. As I recall, we held any number of practices, in preparation for the presentation of our program, and much of the conversation during those preceding weeks centered around who had learned their "pieces," and how many lines each of had "to say."

In addition to involvement in practices, we dreamed of a new outfit for the program, and there was always much speculation about whether the family budget could be expanded to include new shoes. Some years we would proudly sport new patent leather shoes, glistening in their newness and so slippery that we felt we had to "practice walking." Other years, we would polish our school shoes and try to pretend that we did not care.

The young folks of today will not believe this, but an important factor in our Christmas program was attempting to get the church heated sufficiently. This was not an easy task, since the "heating plant" consisted of a large oversized barrel-type stove, placed near the rear of the church. Participants in the program sat near the front of the church, all decked out in their new Christmas finery, which was "very grand," but hardly adequate for the winter weather.

Throughout the winter, we attended Sunday School classes dressed in snowsuits or heavy coats and jackets, but Christmas was the time for getting "all dressed up," no matter how far the mercury was scrunched down in the thermometer. It was a delicate matter to keep the fire going as hot as possible without overheating the stove, and when the stove began to turn a dangerous reddish color at times, it was an indication that the person tending the fire had thrown in one log too many.

The programs were always held in the evenings, with the church beautifully decorated. It was a matter of great pride that the Christmas tree touched the ceiling. Candles and boughs decorated the windows.

We left home with a million instructions ringing in our ears. Don't fidget on the stage, speak clearly, speak loudly enough for everyone to hear, don't slouch, don't giggle, don't tug at your hair ribbon, don't forget your "piece," don't you dare scuff your new shoes, be sure that your stockings aren't wrinkled (they were the long cotton stockings, white for Christmas for the girls and the usual tan for the boys), don't put your fingers in your mouth, don't trip on the step up to the stage, don't run up to the stage, etc. We rehearsed our "pieces" several last times, terrified that we would forget the lines at the crucial moment and disgrace our parents and grandparents forever.

The programs of today seem to go so smoothly, with each child performing beautifully. Not so when I was young. Most of us contributed in some way to "spoiling" the program. There was always the shy little darling who spoke her "piece" in a whisper and stumbled off the stage. Then the little boy whose parents had continually admonished him to "speak up," who hurried on stage, shouted his verse until his face was red and his voice broke, gave a big smile of satisfaction and clumped off to his place in the pew. Another would hurry to the "X" where we were supposed to stand, mutter "Merry Christmstal-Installagduie," and, in terror, flee to her seat. Then another would manage to negotiate the space between his seat and the stage and then stand there and giggle. The teacher would patiently remind him of his "piece," but nothing could stem his laughter. His parents sat in anguish in the audience, until often his father would speak up and sternly tell the giggler to sit down. He would return to his seat, but by then the entire Sunday School was caught up in the spirit of things and everyone was giggling.

Always, each year, there was at least one adorable little doll who would approach the stage with hesitating steps, turn and face the audience, put her head down—and stand there, twirling the hem of her dress. After giving her a sufficient length of time to remember her lines, the teacher would coach, "Merry—." The child would squirm, put her finger in her mouth, and the teacher would repeat the magic word which was suppose to restore the child's speech. Still nothing. "Merry Christmas—," the teacher would further assist. Finally, after the teacher had patiently repeated each word of the verse, with absolutely no response from the child, the teacher would approach the stage, take the child's hand and lead her to her seat. Out in the entrance after the program, the embarrassed parents would have the child repeat her "piece" for as many as would listen, just to prove that she had learned it.

And then, there were the few children who walked gracefully to the stage, faced the audience with cherubic grins, spoke their "pieces" in clear voices, remembered every line of the lengthy verses and, in smug self-satisfaction, leave the stage at just the proper pace. They did everything so well you wanted to give them a good kick in the shins! These were the same children who never tore their trousers, never wrinkled their dresses, never scuffed their shoes, never lost their hair ribbons and raised their hands to answer every single question the teachers in school asked.

The last number on the Christmas program always was the nativity scene, with the shepherds dressed in their father's striped bathrobes, Mary attired in her mother's white flannel nightgown, with a blue sash tied elegantly around her waist to disguise the true nature of her garb, and the other members of this touching tableau vivant wearing various items of clothing borrowed from their parents. It took a great deal of imagination to picture this as the manger scene, in spite of the straw which littered the stage and the crude cradle which held a doll.

After "Silent Night" was sung, the good part of the program arrived—distribution of the treats, a little box of candy with a white string as a handle. In spite of warnings and threats that the boxes were not to be opened, almost all of us could not resist the temptation, and the predicted disaster always happened—the contents of the boxes tipped onto the floor. There lay the peanuts in their shells, mingled with those nauseating cone-shaped chocolate vanilla creams, covered with little pieces of peanut shells.

Back home, the evening was not over until our parents had reviewed our part in the program, either condemning us or praising us, depending upon our performances. Grateful and happy that the ordeal was over for another year, we settled down to shell the peanuts, the only treats we had been allowed to retrieve from the floor.

MATTHEW 1:21—*And she shall bring forth a son, and thou shalt call his name Jesus; for he shall save his people from their sins.*

Chapter 19

Before the year draws to a close, I probably should start thinking of New Year's resolutions—for the current year, of course. There is definitely not time for me to perform a total make-over and certainly not time, even given a century, to start correcting all my faults, so I will limit myself to one resolution. I am going to resolve to do my Christmas shopping early. This decision was actually forced on me by a long-suffering family, who has spent far too many hectic holiday sessions stumbling through ribbons, tinsel, gifts, greeting cards, cookie dough, etc.

I am hereby notifying all the other members of the "League of Last-Minute Shoppers" that I will not be presiding at our annual meeting at the gift counters at 4:00 p.m. on December 24. Oh, I probably will show up for a few last-minute gifts, but I hope to have almost all of our Christmas shopping done before that. I am going to prove to my family that I can be as efficient as everyone else. Well, not everyone else. There are some people whose efficiency is downright disgusting!

Speaking of Christmas shopping, I think it is interesting to note the various kinds of shoppers. First of all, there is the shopper who has had all of her Christmas shopping done, the packages wrapped and mailed or delivered. I can never quite figure out just what she is doing browsing around through the stores, loudly proclaiming to anyone who will listen that her shopping is all done. What is she doing in everyone's way? I have two theories.

One, she really misses the camaraderie and the excitement of that frantic, last-minute scramble for gifts and she joins us serious shoppers to share those memorable moments with us. Or—and I hate to say this when we all should be thinking, "Peace on earth and goodwill to men"—the most likely explanation of her presence in the shops is to stand there and gloat at the desperate struggles of those who have let their shopping go until an hour before the stores are ready to close. The latter theory is more plausible, judging by the smug, self-satisfied, sickening grin on her perfectly cosmeticed (new word, people—write it down!) face.

My favorite shopper is the dear little boy or girl who is looking for gifts for Mommy or Daddy. Nothing is quite as touching. They cautiously examine item after item, shyly inquiring about the price of each one, wanting with all their hearts to find something which will please their mothers and fathers. When they have lovingly made their decisions, they watch, eyes glowing, as the clerk wraps their purchases in gay paper and bright ribbon. They still harbor a little uncertainty about their selection and almost invariably they mumble, "I hope Mommy and Daddy like their presents." If they only knew! They could give Mother a tie and Dad a lipstick, and their parents would still treasure their gifts, realizing the love and devotion behind the presents.

A reminder: Be sure to send greeting cards to all of our hospitalized residents, as well as our people in nursing homes. Those in hospitals are bound to feel isolated and removed from the holiday flurry and excitement. We can all help to cheer them up by showing them that they are remembered and that we care. It is just a small gesture, but you can be sure that it will be deeply appreciated.

I have heard a number of theories about Christmas greeting cards lately. Many say that the practice of sending Christmas greetings is becoming so commercialized, that there is no longer any warmth and friendliness in the gesture—merely a sense of duty. Now, I do not hold to that theory at all! To me, sending and receiving cards is one of the nicest practices of Christmas.

Hearing from old friends, many of whom we hear from only at Christmas, always means a lot to me. As one Tower reader said, "Receiving a card from a relative or friend is something like sharing our Christmas with them." My personal experience last year when I did not send Christmas cards taught me an invaluable lesson. Last year during the Christmas season, as cards arrived from people who have touched our lives, I felt more and more guilty. I did not deserve their greetings. Some of them were far busier than I, but they took the time to send a card and note to us. I was riddled with shame and guilt. Never again! As long as I can hold a pen and write somewhat legibly, I will send Christmas cards.

When I first made my "NO Christmas Cards" decision last year, Jim was all for it. He was ecstatic. I definitely had brightened his holidays! However, as the cards began to come in with messages to keep us abreast of the happenings in the lives of those who mean so much, Jim became more and more doubtful of the wisdom of my decision. It was not long before he actually remembered (???) that he mentioned (??) that it was not a good idea when I first broached the subject.

With all of our other Christmas activities, we must not forget the most important thing—the real reason for Christmas. Take time to observe Christmas in the manner in which it was first intended. Attend the place of worship of your choice.

"You aren't really as bad about last-minute Christmas preparations as you say, are you?" a reader asked this week, in total disbelief. I hesitated, debating whether or not I should tell the truth, but we never know when Santa is listening at this time of the year, so I admitted, in all honesty, "Worse—much worse than I would ever admit!" My disorganized holiday preparations might seem humorous to you readers, but to me, it is almost pathetic.

The Christmas spirit takes possession of me the day before Christmas, and brimming over with increased love for everyone, I frantically try to express my devotion by telephoning friends, just to let them know I am thinking of them. I am sure they could not care less, when they themselves are scurrying around, attending to last-minute details. I insist that folks wend their way through papers, boxes, decorations, ribbon and tinsel to share a cup of coffee with me and to sample my first batch of Christmas cookies—if they would only settle down, sit back and wait a few minutes (what is their hurry, for goodness' sake?) for the cookies to come out of the oven. I ignore the clerk's offer to gift-wrap my last-minute purchases, and entangled in ribbon, seals, and wrapping paper, fumble through my gift-wrapping, enveloped completely in a feeling of self-satisfaction, coupled, of course, with a great deal of panic. So—from all of us at The Tower News—we wish each of you a Blessed Christmas and much happiness, success and peace in the New Year. We thank you all for your support, your loyalty, your encouragement and your assistance. You are remarkable people and we appreciate every one of you!

LUKE 2:11—For unto you is born this day in the city of David a Savior, who is Christ the Lord.

Chapter 20

On Saturday, Jim announced that the weather was ideal for a snowmobile ride—my chance to get a ride on his new secondhand machine. Now, we're not talking Taconite Trail or a ride to Cook or Virginia. With me plunked on the back of a snowmobile, a "ride" is of no more than an hour's duration, and never so far from home that I can't walk back, just in case Jim gets disgusted enough to dump me off in a snowbank.

Our destination was "Face Rock," which won't mean anything to those under fifty years of age. I was led to believe that Face Rock (somewhere on a hill behind Tower) was a sight which very few people are privileged to experience in a lifetime. I'll admit that the view was spectacular, truly breathtaking. One could see for miles and miles and it was gorgeous. Face Rock itself is supposed to border on somewhat of a religious experience, I guess. Try as I might, I could not discern a face on that rock, but maybe erosion over the past hundred years or so has taken its toll. Or maybe I was not viewing the rock from the right angle.

In addition to the beautiful panoramic view, I was treated to a lesson on topography. Fortunately, there was no quiz, because I did not retain a single fact. This ridge extends to there, that valley winds around to there, this lies behind the Tower airport, this continues onto wherever. I never have been able to visualize such things. I did see Soudan—recognized it without any help—and Jasper Peak and the Soudan Mine Hill. It was a nice "trip," and Jim complimented me when we got home. "For once," he said, "you didn't spend the entire time complaining." (I guess he couldn't hear over the roar of the snowmobile, but I accepted the compliment graciously.)

JOHN 15:1—*I am the true vine, and my Father is the husbandman.*

Chapter 21

"One would think that if the fish weren't caught on opening day, they would all vanish from the lake," I wrote in a column last week. Well, guess who was out fishing Saturday morning. Fishing on opening day was a new experience for me. It was like a carnival. So much for the peace and tranquility of the outdoors and getting back to nature! There was never a second that one didn't hear the drone or roar of a motor. The Narrows was literally crowded with boats, with estimates ranging from one hundred to two hundred watercraft of every description. There were canoes, rowboats, fishing boats, pontoon boats, houseboats, cruisers, yachts, boats with flying bridges—you name it.

People were shouting back and forth, there was the constant babble of conversation and laughter. One young fellow fell in the lake and his fishing companions had a time getting him back in the boat.

Boats were running over people's fishing lines, and one fellow managed to get a fishing line securely wrapped around his boat propeller before the line broke. He spent the next half hour getting the line from the propeller, with some young fellows in an adjacent boat assisting him.

I caught a walleye so small that it had to be returned to his mother. I caught a couple of other fish, but they got away before I could see what they were. My husband maintains, of course, that one does not CATCH a fish unless one has it in the boat. That is ridiculous. I catch fish, but they just get away.

My next catch was a Northern, and I learned that one is not supposed to catch Northerns. "How can I help it if they bite my hook?" I argued. "I didn't come out here to argue," my fisherman husband said firmly. "I came out to relax and enjoy myself. I'm telling you we don't want Northerns."

I grabbed another candy bar and meditated as I munched. Why is it that ardent fishermen marry lukewarm-to-cool fisherwomen? Why do rock music fans marry persons who enjoy only symphony music? Why do mountain climbers marry bookworms? Why do—the lapping of the waves, the warm sunshine and the gentle motion of the boat lulled me to sleep as soon as I finished my candy bar.

I was awakened by a strong tug on my line. "A fish," I screamed. "I've got a big fish!" I had a big one, all right—about 150 pounds! The fellow in the next boat had hooked onto my line. We got that all straightened out, but he soon repeated the maneuver.

A boatload of fellows, with more enthusiasm than talent, broke into a chorus of "Roll Out the Barrel." A wholesome, fresh young girl in the next boat soon succumbed to the fresh air, melted into the bow of the boat, lifted her face to the sun and fell asleep. One arm hung over the boat, but she maintained a firm grasp on her fishing rod with the other hand. I watched, fascinated, as she sat completely limp for over an hour, but never relaxed her hold on her rod.

The wind came up and we drifted a little until we were almost bumping into a big yacht. My line drifted, too, and became entangled in the line of a gentleman on the yacht. It was so embarrassing! "I'm afraid I'm tangled in your line," I said timidly. He was so nice. He actually looked pleasant as he carefully straightened out the lines. I apologized profusely—and then my hat blew off! I fished that out of the water, settled down to fish again, and caught my hook in the anchor rope of the nice man's yacht. My husband tried to help me by letting the boat drift so my line would go slack. No use. "I'm sorry," I stammered to the still-nice man. "I seemed to be caught in your anchor rope." Well, he puffed on his cigar through his smiles, patiently freed my line again, and maintained his composure throughout the humiliating experience.

My husband had had enough. He started the motor and we chugged our way through those millions of boats, homeward bound.

Oh, I forgot to mention that I caught another Northern—Just to show that nobody can tell ME not to catch Northerns.

MATTHEW 5:44—*But I say unto you. Love your enemies, bless them that curse you, do good to them that hate you, and pray for them which despitefully use you, and persecute you.*

Chapter 22

Our neighborhood has become much too quiet. There are no cheery greetings, "Hi, Phyllis!" or "Hi, Jim!" There were tearful farewells this week as our neighbors' grandson, Bryan, returned home, after spending part of the summer here with his grandparents. I choked up as I said goodbye to Bryan, who gave me a big hug, patted my hand, and said in his consoling tone of voice, "It's okay, Phyllis. I'll be back at Christmas. Time goes fast." He gave Jim a big hug and said his farewells. Bryan adds a new dimension to any life he touches. He is seven, going on seventy. A talented artist, he concentrates on drawing birds, and he is remarkable! It was extremely touching to watch this little boy sit, cross-legged, on the shoreline, drawing such perfect pictures of the ducks, they could almost fly right off the paper. (I assured him that I was saving all his drawings, and when he gets to be a very famous artist, I will be rich!) Bryan felt that it was his duty to keep these ducks fed, and he was thrilled when they got accustomed to him and would run up to him for food.

He recognizes even the most unusual species of birds, and would often try to enlighten me—"this is the Eastern bluebird," "this is the cross-billed cuckoo." He spent many hours capturing ants and building homes for them—and the ants seemed content in their new environment. He tirelessly would study their habits for hours. He later released them, with my cautioning him not to free them on our lot.

Bryan enjoys and appreciates nature. On one of our walks, he found a bee which seemed injured. He carefully placed a blossom near the insect, and it crawled up on the blossom, which Bryan tenderly picked up and carried as we continued on the walk. We had gone a considerable distance, planning how Bryan could take care of the bee, when, suddenly, it recovered and flew off, much to Bryan's delight and relief. He had really been concerned about the "sick bee."

"We" later spent at least a half hour trying to throw rocks into a woodpecker hole in a dead tree, but Bryan never lost interest, and the next evening he impatiently waited for me to come home from work, so we "could throw rocks again."

Flowers and weeds are another of Bryan's specialties. He had pots of weeds and flowers in his "fort," and he faithfully nurtured them and watched with satisfaction as they grew. He often carried a potted plant down the steep hill to show us his latest acquisition. He would carefully check Jim's tomato, raspberry and cucumber plants, and was even more excited than Jim when the tomatoes began to ripen and the cucumbers grew to "eating size."

Taking a walk with Bryan would open new worlds for anyone who had the privilege of his company. "We" checked each weed and each anthill and identified every single tree. When we encountered something unfamiliar, Bryan was impatient to get home to check it out in the "tree book," "the weed book" or "the flower book."

Jim and I will never forget one memorable experience, which we have delighted in telling many people. Almost daily, Jim expresses his intense dislike of wiping out the shower stall after he takes a shower. One day, while I was at work, Jim and Bryan were visiting together and he told Bryan that he could not do something or other. I do not even know what it was that Bryan was forbidden to do, but Bryan argued, "Phyllis lets me do it." Jim firmly stated, "I am the boss in this house. What I say goes. Phyllis is not the boss." Bryan, who has extremely expressive eyes, got a strange look in his eyes, and asked, "If you're the boss, how come you have to wipe out the tub?" That's "our" Bryan! We will really miss him.

JOHN 14:18—*I will not leave you comfortless: I will come to you.*

Family Photos

Jim, 1945, after his return from Alaska, where
he served with the U.S. Army for four years.

Jim and Phyllis

Our beautiful mother, Ferne Driscoll

The "newer" linotype which replaced the one that was in the shop when Jin purchased the business. This was used to set the type. It is shown "stripped down" without the "magazines," but was used until 1981, when Jim shutoff the switch for the last time. (Photo by Gary Burgess)

Happiness is . . . successful walleye fishing!

Jim at 87 years of age, returning from a partridge hunt

Pat and Paul Krieg, our daughter and son-in-law

Jim and our daughter Pat—such great pals!

Jim and Bucky II

Her Royal Highness, Queen Jasmine

Chapter 23

Our aging lab, Bucky, reveled in the couple of warm, sunny days with which we were blessed recently. Housebound most of the winter, he was able to lie outside and bask in the sunshine. In deference to his advanced years, he had a heavy blanket beneath him and wore his coat. ("A hunting dog wearing a coat!" Jim scoffed, but Bucky and I relish our creature comforts, and at our age, we like to be warm and cozy.)

In the past years, Bucky has always lain outside, supervising, as Jim goes about his outdoor projects, and he happily resumed his position of command a couple of times during the past week, his tail wagging furiously. Bucky is still a gorgeous, regal animal, with a sleek, glistening coat. When they were young, the daughters of my brother and sister-in-law used the term, "Bucky Black," to describe things that were "the blackest black in the world." Lying down, Bucky is the picture of perfect health, his magnificent head often lifted to catch the slightest scent. He really surveys his kingdom and alertly keeps track of the slightest activity. Tweety birds are completely ignored, scampering squirrels merit a passing glance, snowmobiles command more interest and he charts their course. His ears will perk up at the sight of a large bird standing on the ground, but his trained eye immediately ascertains that it is not a partridge, and he relaxes again. In an upright position, Bucky is still very handsome, but his advancing age is reflected in his sometimes unsteady, halting gait and the weariness which too much exertion sometimes causes.

He has won the heart of many a female Lab over the years. (I just realized, as I mentally was reviewing the list of his admirers, that every one was a blonde.) He still carries on a May—December romance with a beautiful yellow Lab, Brandy, who absolutely adores him, and it is touching to see them together.

All of this leads us to an incident that occurred the other day. Bucky was outside enjoying the sunshine, with me (his care-giver) standing beside him. Suddenly, his ears perked up, his head raised and his body tensed. He focused on a spot about twenty feet from us and remained rigid and motionless. I moved around one vantage point to another, peering around one tree after another, in an attempt to determine what could possibly interest Bucky that much. I have been known to exaggerate—on rare occasions—but when I estimate that Bucky held that pose for several minutes, it is true.

Jim, noting that Bucky was "on the alert," came outside to ask what was claiming our guard dog's attention. When I responded that I had no idea, and that my attempts to see anything had been futile, Jim approached the area. It was at that moment that a beautiful, large mink bounded from under the dock and scampered along the shoreline. Rather than retreating, however, the splendid animal stopped at what it considered a safe distance from us and eyed us curiously. Bucky had not moved a muscle and continued to zero in on the mink. The animal reared its head and raised up to get a better view, and this tableau continued for some time. Finally, the mink stood right up on its hind legs, the white patch of its chest in sharp contrast to its lovely brown coat. After achieving an upright position several times, the mink's curiosity was satisfied, and it loped up the hill. Jim, who has witnessed almost everything there is to see in the woods, said that he has never, ever seen a mink behave like that and had never seen one so bold. Although mink are usually secretive and shy, this mink was fully aware of our presence and evidenced no fear—only curiosity. It was a magical moment, and one I will cherish. To be privileged to share such a scene makes me feel very fortunate.

GENESIS 1:24—*And God said, Let the earth being forth the living creatures after his kind, cattle, and creeping things, and beast of the earth after his kind; and it was so.*

Chapter 24

It was inevitable. Our marriage has gone through countless phases: Fishing, hunting, snowmobiling, flying an airplane, windsledding, fly tying, speed boat racing—you name it. Naturally, I am not the participant, merely the observer. So, when my daughter and her husband got motorcycles—yes, that's right, WE got a motorcycle.

Saturday was set as the day when I would go for a motorcycle ride—as a passenger, of course.

Let me explain. I am a chicken. I wear a life vest in the bathtub. I tie lifelines when I ascend more than two rungs on a ladder. The most dangerous action I ever undertake is to cross a street.

After the helmet is donned, I get my instructions. Put your feet here, and keep them there. (Would I move them?) Hang on here. Relax. (Relax? Is he crazy?) Off we go—to a bad start. As he is shifting gears, my helmet clangs against his helmet. "I've had it," I think. Above the panic and the ringing in my ears, I hear him shouting, "Keep your head back when I'm shifting, woman." Now, how am I supposed to know when he is going to shift gears?

We take off at the breathtaking speed of twenty miles an hour. Do I dare ask him to slow down? This eternally young husband already feels that he is married to a great-grandmother—an overly cautious one, at that. "Look around, relax, enjoy yourself," he advises. I hang on for dear life and stare straight ahead at the design on his helmet, thinking that grasping the bar under the seat would scarcely save me if we tipped over. Somehow the center of gravity doesn't seem right.

We sail along and after some time he shouts, "We're going fifty miles an hour." "Slow down, slow down," I scream. There is one thing about this motorcycling—it is almost impossible to carry on a decent argument above the noise.

I find myself tucking my legs in tightly whenever we meet an approaching car. I somehow have the feeling that my knees are sticking out into the other lane.

We travel along the less frequented roads, with my spouse gleefully zipping along, shifting gears. He looks from side to side, enjoying the scenery, pointing out places of interest. "So–and–so lives there." "Look at that beautiful horse. What a beautiful animal." "The tree must be a hundred years old." Finally, I can stand it no longer. Above the noise of the machine, I scream, "Please, please keep your eyes on the road!"

It was at this point that we began the homeward journey, and I finally found myself safe in the back yard. I painfully pried each finger from the bars and it took only a couple of hours before I could bend my arms again.

His eyes shone with happiness and pride as he invited, "Now, any time you want to ride, just let me know. I'll be glad to take you any time!" "As soon as I get over this," I think as I stumble towards the house.

MATTHEW 22:14—*For many are called, but few are chosen.*

Chapter 25

He died as he had lived—with dignity. Snikker had been a member of my sister's family for almost sixteen years, during which he brought much happiness, more than a little excitement, and of course some anxiety at times, into their lives. He was a medium size, tan dog—or four-legged person, whichever you prefer. I think that Snikker, realizing the faults and shortcomings of people, would want to be considered a dog. He had none of the pettiness or vindictiveness characteristic of humans. (Now, jealousy, that is a different story.)

Snikker gave added dimension to the meaning of devotion. He was a dear, faithful, loyal pet. He maintained a superior and condescending attitude toward the poodles which became members of the family during his reign. When the blue heeler arrived, his approach was much different and he seemed to view Fred as a threat. Eventually, they worked things out between them, probably because Fred deferred to Snikker's advanced age and years of experience.

He grew up with the three children, sharing their lives as they advanced from tricycles to wagons to bicycles to cars and trucks. He was seldom far from them.

Snikker was not without his feisty side, however. He did not want another animal invading his territory. "He was a scrapper," my nephew observed with affection, "and he seldom lost a fight." When he did, he came inside, humiliated and bleeding—but undaunted, just the same.

We all recall countless incidents in which Snikker showed his unique, special personality (dogality?). As we grieved for him on Saturday, we could summon up laughter as we recalled the time Pris' husband was on the garage roof, making repairs, and he turned around to see Snikker beside him. Snikker had, indeed, climbed up the ladder. Getting down was not so simple, but just to show that he could do it, Snikk ascended the ladder again.

He accompanied my nephew on his newspaper route years ago and knew the route as well as my nephew. When he was still quite young, he was wounded by gunshot and lost the sight of one eye. He adjusted well, but the injury made him more defensive. In later years, his hearing began to fail, and on one occasion this caused us much anxiety. He had accompanied a group of young people, including my nephew, across the ice-frozen lake and, as usual, had romped around happily as they worked, clearing an area of brush. When it came time to come home, Snikker had disappeared. The young people concluded that he had decided to find his way home. They were dismayed later to discover that Snikker had not preceded them home. Everyone spent some anxious hours searching, realizing that their calls were falling, literally, on deaf ears. He returned home that evening, haughty and indignant at having been "deserted," but nevertheless, willing to forgive.

He was loved by the neighbors, as well as by all of us. He would visit Vickie and the Haskells and, of course, Grandma next door. Grandma and her friend, Bethel, seldom went walking without Snikker at their heels. Bethel, too, loved "Ripper," as she called him. My sister's tiny granddaughter adored Snikker and he patiently and lovingly endured her displays of affection, even when she occasionally got a bit too rough.

My sister spent much of Saturday with her beloved pet. Silently communicating, they both understood, as she stopped frequently to talk to him and pet him, that they were spending some of his last hours together. They had a very special time on Saturday. Then, as I said, Snikker went out into the back entry, laid down, and with dignity, quietly died. We'll never forget him.

LUKE 21:33—*Heaven and earth shall pass away; but my words shall not pass away.*

Chapter 26

Seven of us women who had graduated from high school together met recently to honor one of the seven who was retiring (an early, early retirement, of course). These were the same girls who had giggled their way through discussions on "cute" boys, opinions on the songs on the jukeboxes in Tregear's and Marttila's, grades on our report cards, new hair styles, new fashions in clothes, movies and leading movie stars of that era.

The rapid passage of time was never as pronounced as it was that evening. We exchanged symptoms of our aches and pains, discussed doctors and surgical operations, and assured each other that we did not feel even a year older than we did at graduation.

In what had to have been the classic example of precision movement, as the menus were placed on the table, five of us simultaneously reached into our handbags and in the same instant, as if rehearsed, put on our eyeglasses. (The other two women were already wearing theirs.)

The subject of "cute" boys was replaced with accounts of cute stories of the grandchildren. The only time the subject of clothes came up was during a discussion of the types of clothes which hide our bulges, bags and wrinkles. We are still concerned about our hair, but forget the latest hair styles. Now, all we want to know is how to cover up the gray.

The last movie stars any of us had heard of were Elizabeth Taylor and Clark Gable. Movies? Do they STILL have theatres?

We studied the menu endlessly, seeking foods which "agree" with us, interrupting each other's perusal of the carte du jour with comments on our success (or lack thereof) with our current diets.

We reminisced about our high school days, the teachers, the coaches, the ball teams. Those were topics we really enjoyed. It did get frustrating, however. Who was the coach after Miller? Was it Vern Miller? What subject did Ellen Swanson teach? Who was the teacher who wore the unusual boots? Who taught social studies? Was it Mr. Norsted—Melvin Norsted? Fortunately, between the seven of us, we managed to get most of the questions answered.

The atmosphere became solemn as we recalled the class members who have died. It is very sobering to note that the list keeps getting longer and longer.

Whoever would have thought that the same girls who had not harbored a single constructive thought throughout their high school years were now discussing recipes, handwork, the economy and household hints?

One carryover from our high school days was our sense of humor. We still giggled and laughed throughout the evening.

As the evening wore on and we finally had to say our farewells, another factor became evident. We had spent our high school years conscientiously observing the curfews set by our parents. In those days, there was no thought of punishment for coming in after the designated curfew. There just was no such thing as missing a curfew.

So—after all these years we could wander home whenever we liked? Hardly! Now, we had husbands waiting at home for us. We emphatically assured each other that we were liberated, modern women, but we "must hurry home now, so Jim (or Charles or Dick or Stan) would not worry about us." Time sometimes changes only the characters, not the scene.

PSALM 116:9—*I will walk before the Lord in the land of the living.*

Chapter 27

Hearts are heavy in Tower-Soudan this week, and the undercurrent of grief and sadness cannot be fully overcome. As businessmen go about their work, as students pursue their studies, as housewives attend to their thousands of demanding tasks and as men go to their daily jobs, the feeling continues to persist. It started last Sunday morning when Mrs. Raymond Burgess responded to the ring of a doorbell and opened her door to an official from the U.S. Army. The man's presence spoke for itself, and she knew that the months of worry, despair and apprehension were over—ended in a manner which families of servicemen hold in dread and fear.

The Raymond Burgess family was fully aware of the dangers involved in the type of combat in which their son, Specialist Four Dick Burgess, participated. Every family of a serviceman is forced to consider the possibility that they might open their door to an official someday. Yet each family prays that the day will never come.

During World War II a number of families in Tower-Soudan received the dreaded news, conveyed differently in those days, but with the same meaning. Perhaps our communities' having given so many sons during that conflict made us believe that we held some sort of an immunity now. Every week the daily newspapers have carried articles of death in Viet Nam, and because Tower-Soudan is as one big family, we mentally review the names of our boys serving in Viet Nam, and say a little prayer for their safety. Now, the dreaded phrase, "killed in action," has hit home, and Tower-Soudan finds it most difficult to face. Even the very young, not fully aware of the gravity of the situation, can sense that "something is, indeed, wrong."

Dick Burgess was one of our popular young men. Everyone "loves life," as the worn-out phrase goes, but Dick's love of life was manifest in so many ways—his intense interest in everything, his zest and enthusiasm for a wide range of activities. Interested in music, he organized a band, which he promoted in a number of ways. Interested in mechanics, he undertook the task of "rebuilding" a car. Interested in the out-of-doors, he industriously set about to raze an old home and salvage the materials for a "shack" in the woods. He was constantly "on the go," wringing the most out of each precious minute.

And who will ever forget those sparkling hazel eyes, which continued to twinkle even when he wasn't smiling? Handsome, happy-go-lucky, enthusiastic, he had only to smile to win one's heart.

Dick had been counting the days until his return home, had made plans for his summer. It all came to an end last Wednesday, when "hostile fire" took one of our beloved Tower-Soudan sons. Not the first, we fully realize, to die for his country on foreign soil, but how deep the pain, how acute the sense of loss when he is "our boy."

This heart-wrenching scene was repeated several months later when the family of Nicholas Stefanich endured the same experiences, "Nicky," too, having paid the supreme sacrifice in Viet Nam.

EPHESIANS 6:24—*Grace be with all them that love our Lord Jesus Christ in sincerity. Amen.*

Chapter 28

In the light of recent events, as the worn-out saying goes, I have come to the conclusion that there is great need for at least one addition to the literary field. I am sure that there are thousands of "How To" books, including "How to Feed an Albatross While Standing on Your Head" (I'm not sure if the albatross is standing on the person's head, or if the person himself is doing a headstand) and "How To Peel a Banana If You're Left-handed." A field sadly neglected and a volume for which there must be a sizable market would be "How to Assume an Air of Innocence at a Police Station."

This touchy subject would probably have to be handled in two sections—when you really are innocent, and when you are guilty. A recent car accident in which I was involved convinced me that such a book is a definite necessity. Fortunately, I was the innocent party in the mishap, but it seems that this fact does not exclude a person from the unnerving experience of a visit to the police station.

Before I go on, I want to impress on you the fact that I have what I consider a more-than-average respect for law enforcement officers. Some of my good friends are members of the police force, and I do not want you to think that I do not have the proper regard for the important and often thankless tasks they perform. They have my deepest respect, and I mean that sincerely.

Well, at any rate, the policeman very nicely asked me if I would drive down to the police station. No handcuffs, no ride in the police car, with the sirens screaming—just a very courteous request to come to the station. As I sneaked up the steps leading into the building, I prayed that nobody "from home" would happen to recognize me. Then began an endless tour of the rooms—Juvenile Department (that was DEFINITELY OUT!)—Chief of Police (let's hope that this incident didn't have to be taken that high up)—Traffic Bureau (that sounded more like it)—then I came to an open door and a man behind the high desk asked if he could help me. I blushed as I informed him that I was told to come down to the police station. "About that accident?" he asked. I was shocked by the fact that even HE already knew about it. He invited me to sit down on a long bench just inside the door and wait until the officer "working on the case" came back. All those television programs centering around police stations began crowding my mind with an alarming clarity. I stumbled to the bench and sat down woodenly. "I'm completely innocent!" I reassured myself. The man at the desk went back to reading his newspaper, and I was left with my thoughts. "Perhaps if I try to look extremely dignified, everyone will know I am innocent," I mused.

Then I decided, after an embarrassingly long interval, that I might be overdoing the "dignified bit," and maybe I was, instead, giving the impression of indifference and hardened unconcern for the whole proceedings. A janitor appeared on the scene and decided that the area in front of the open door had been sadly neglected. Apparently, he was trying to wipe away the entire varnished surface as he concentrated his efforts on the area just outside the door—and concentrated his attention, so it seemed, on me. I detected scorn and disgust in his frequent glances, and I assure you that it was with a great deal of effort that I suppressed the strong desire to explain the whole situation to him and proclaim my innocence!

Trying to ignore the janitor, I turned my attention to the opposite wall, which was literally papered with those "Wanted" bulletins. One

104

interested me especially—a picture of a very good-looking man, with the caption, "Please help me find my brother." For want of anything better to do, I went over to look at the bulletin more closely. The policeman, who had been deeply involved with his newspaper, suddenly snapped to attention, "D'ya think you know him? Have you seen him?" The last of my composure shattered. "What makes him think I would know one of these criminals—I'm only here to fill out an accident report!" I protested silently. I stammered some reply, and felt called upon to give a reason for my close scrutiny of the poster— but thought better of it, recalling the old saying about "protesting too much." I felt a little heartened when, upon reading the bulletin, I discovered that the man was not a criminal after all, but a noted scientist who had disappeared. At least the policeman had evidently not been implying that I was associated with criminals.

The man behind the desk either finished reading his newspaper or decided that the atmosphere was not conducive to reading—and it was with mixed feelings that I watched him carefully fold the paper and turn his attention to me. Days ago (or so it seemed) when I first walked into the room, I would have been grateful for someone to talk with—now I was not too certain that conversation was what I needed, after all. He was a very pleasant fellow, however—understanding and courteous, and I began to feel more at ease. Before I had completely "pulled myself together," however, the moment I had been dreading arrived, in the person of the policeman "on the case."

Now let me tell you something about those television programs. They may exaggerate, they may mislead, they may dramatize—but one thing they portray to perfection. That's the calm, cool attitude— bordering on nonchalance—with which officers of the law handle situations. However, there the similarity ended. The reports were filled in quietly and with almost an air of detachment. No third degree, no being seated on a chair with a bright light in your face, surrounded by policemen. In fact, the officer did not even once question the truth of our statements. (By now the other party in the case

105

had arrived, of course.) He asked each question in the very friendliest manner, wrote down our answers without hesitation—in general, he just could not have been nicer. In fact, the action proceeded so smoothly that I began to get just a little suspicious—could it be that this was just the preliminary and routine procedure, and the Third Degree would come later? Perish the thought! The reports were finished, the other party had furnished his bail money, the time he had to appear in court was set, and we stood fearfully awaiting the "Next Step." The policeman retired to his desk to complete the reports, and we anxiously shuffled by the high counter—speaking in whispers. Suddenly he looked up, amazed to see us all standing there, and said, "Well, you can go any time you want!" I hesitated, positive that I had heard wrong, but the other people headed swiftly for the door, and I almost stumbled over them in my eagerness to leave the premises!

Looking back, I know that my shattered composure left no room for sensible reasoning, and the incident took on huge proportions in my mind. Had I approached the situation with a clearer, more sane attitude, I would not have become so shaken by the whole unpleasantness. I pray that there isn't a "Next Time," but if there ever should be—well, I'm sorry but I must admit that I will probably react the same way again.

PROVERBS 29:18—*Where there is no vision, the people perish; but he that keepeth the law, happy is he.*

106

Chapter 29

Did this ever happen to you? You get up some morning, feeling sleepy and grouchy. You sit on the edge of the bed and moodily reflect on the injustice of being forced to arise so early in the morning. The mere thought of the regular morning routine of dressing, shaving, showering, etc. seems to exhaust you. You pass your hand a safe one-half inch from your face to "test" your beard? Well, now, that proves you don't need a shave—not even the slightest scratchiness.

Now, this act sets the pattern for the entire day. A chain reaction sets in. The T-shirt you pull from the drawer has a frayed neckline—well, no matter. Your trousers could stand a pressing—but you'll wear them one more time. Now, how about a sport shirt, so you can get by without a tie? The shirt you wrestle out of the closet has a slight tear at the edge of the pocket, but the effort of hanging it up again would be too great, so you slip into it. You are now set for the day.

With a start like this, things are just bound to get worse. Your ball point pen leaks in your shirt pocket, mayonnaise from your noon sandwich leaves an ugly, dark spot on your trousers—but there is a bright spot in your day. You happen along just as that beautiful, shapely blonde down the block discovers she has a flat tire. Feeling every bit the hero, you expertly change the tire, while she coos about now strong, intelligent and handsome you are. So, as you gallantly

107

continue on your way, the grime resulting from the tire change becomes a mark of distinction in your mind.

Where will this all end? Well, I'll tell you. Make no mistake about it. One of two events will take place as sure as the sun rises in the morning and sets each evening. You will, without a doubt, meet a favorite old girlfriend, whom you haven't seen in twenty years. She will look exactly as she did when she used to rest her beautiful head on your shoulder and tell you how handsome, neat, efficient and wonderful you were. Or—perish the thought—you will meet your wife's old boyfriend—the one who now heads a big company, dresses like Robert Taylor (even looks a little bit like him) and probably (you tell yourself bitterly) would rather buy a new car than stop to change a tire. So men—remember that next time you decide not to shave!

2 CHRONICLES 6:42—*O Lord God, turn not away the face of thine anointed; remember the mercies of David thy servant.*

Chapter 30

Saturday started out as an "okay" day. It was the opening of fishing season, the weather was tolerable and I was grateful that I could be outdoors getting some of my chores done. It was quite a bit like any other day until about four o'clock, when a huge flatbed truck eased into our narrow driveway. This was an anticipated event, but I had been pushing it to the back of my mind and since I did not know exactly when it would happen, I had been ignoring it for several days.

One of my quirks is giving human traits to some of the inanimate objects in my life. My refrigerator, my clothes dryer, my clothes washer have personalities and have become parts of my life. For some strange reason, I have never felt a close bond with my stove. As the huge truck made its way down the driveway, my eyes filled with tears. What had I done to one of the most faithful objects in my life? How could I have been so cold-hearted, so uncaring, so very ungrateful? Is that how one rewards years of service? Is that how one expresses gratitude?

I do have to credit myself for making every effort to restore it to good health. I had taken drastic measures and had turned a deaf ear when family and friends told me "it was time." My stomach knotted and turned to ice as the truck driver lined his vehicle up with the stall in the garage. I felt like wailing loudly and throwing myself dramatically across the hood of my beloved car. How could I even have harbored the thought of parting with it? I watched the entire procedure with a sinking heart. My "limousine!" What would the driver of the flatbed have done if I told him that I had changed my mind? My proud station wagon looked so pitiful, so vulnerable as it was being winched on to the flat bed. I know it felt alone, abandoned and disgraced. This could not be happening to us! That gorgeous, regal vehicle, the epitome of dependability. It had never really let me down, and this is how I rewarded it.

Jim had bought the sleek, handsome station wagon second-hand and a couple of days after its purchase, we went on a pheasant hunting trip to South Dakota. Jim and Bucky took care of the hunting; I took care of Jim and Bucky. Once in a while I would have to join Bucky in a field to "hunt 'em up" as the second bird dog. I was walking along a farm road one day while Jim and Bucky were out hunting, and two men in a vehicle stopped and started to chat. "That your Pontiac wagon a couple of miles back?" one of the men asked. I answered that my husband did have a station wagon, but I did not think it was a Pontiac. I rejoined Jim later and checked on the make of the vehicle—of course, a Pontiac. That is how much I was involved in the purchase of this station wagon. Jim handled all such transactions and made the decisions, although I usually got a chance to look at a vehicle before he bought it. When I told Jim about the conversation with the men, he was embarrassed for me and disgusted that I did not at least know the make of the car. That was our first and last hunting trip out of state with the Pontiac wagon. At the time, of course, we had no inkling that we would never be hunting out there again.

This Pontiac became Jim's car, ideal for hunting and fishing and towing his snowmobile, ATV or even a lawnmower or other piece of equipment that had to be taken in for repair. Quite a few years later, when Jim purchased a brand new car, the ownership of the station wagon gradually shifted over to me. It was the perfect vehicle to drive the three miles to work. It would start in thirty or forty below weather, after having been parked outside all day. It was heavy and determined to please and would bravely navigate through many inches of snow.

The cancerous rust spots started to spread to take over the doors and Jim considered having body work done on it, but when he checked on the possibility, he was told it was no longer possible. He had waited too long. (The medical term is "terminal.") To me, that wagon was still beautiful and wonderful. The controls to the door locks and windows on the driver's door popped out of their console, so I used duct tape to seal them back in, replacing the tape when necessary. I adjusted to all the little idiosyncrasies of the vehicle, as it uncomplainingly adjusted to mine. We were a good pair.

In time, the passenger door would not open from the inside, so I had to get out, run around the front of the car and release the passenger, using the handle on the outside of the door. After Jim was gone, there was scarcely ever a passenger, so no problem.

Then one day a couple of months ago, the door on the driver's side locked and nothing would budge it, so I had to gain access to the car from the passenger side. Graceful I am not! Getting in the car at home alone in the garage posed no problem, but clumsily exiting the car on Tower's Main Street was not a sight to which I wanted to subject anyone. I made arrangements with Bob of Bob's Amoco to get the door unlocked, but I never seemed to get the car into his garage. After it sat in our garage during weeks of cold, windy weather, I tried to start the vehicle. It faithfully responded immediately and I patted it affectionately. However, a couple of days later, when I went to drive it to Bob's, the engine would not even turn over. My nephew charged the battery and called me at work to tell me that my car was ready to go. Everything would have been fine (I think) if I had taken the car into Bob's that day, but I waited a couple of days, and the battery was dead again. In a moment of insanity, I buckled under the pressure I had been receiving from friends and family for a couple of years and made the horrible decision. My heart aches every time I see that empty, gaping space in the garage.

No one else seems disturbed by the "passing" of the car. My sister was ecstatic and matter-of-fact. My daughter flippantly remarked, "You should have done it a couple of years ago." My brother-in law, knowing how much that car meant to me, tempered his statement with sympathy and friends spoke of the car's demise in jest.

The "newer" car is haughty, arrogant, smug, critical and does not have a single loyal wheel on its frame. I just cannot see our ever having a close relationship. It is better this way.

1 JOHN 3:8—*He that comitteth sin is one of the devil, for the devil sinneth from the beginning. For this purpose the Son of God was manifested, that he might destroy the works of the devil.*

Chapter 31

Jim was outside while I was hanging the wash on the line the other day. I had several batches to hang, so even though the batches were in separate baskets and I had tried to organize the pieces before I began the task of hanging the clothes, it was a little more complicated than usual. I occasionally rearranged the pieces I had already hung to keep them "grouped" properly. When Jim could stand it no longer, he questioned the logic of such a procedure. "What does it matter if all the pillow cases are together? The clothes are hung, they dry, and in a couple of hours you take them down, and only you know that everything was not hung together." A typical male, he demanded an explanation for this complicated procedure of hanging clothes—not just by grouping, but also by color in each grouping. For instance, the white pillow cases are hung first and the remaining pillow cases are hung by color, with the pastels next and continuing on to the darker colors.

"Why? What difference does it make?" he questioned. "Because," I answered, assuming that my firm emphasis on that single word would explain the logic of the situation. Female logic and male logic bear no resemblance to each other, however. (Is there such as thing as male logic?) Jim was not "buying" that explanation, and he pursued the topic. "Because, that is just the way it is," I argued, enunciating each word very clearly. He interrupted by taking exception to the way

I was hanging the sheets and then went on to criticize the fact that I insist that the pajamas must be hung in order—top, bottom, top, bottom, top, bottom. We have been married far too long for either of us to back down on such a serious, earthshaking matter, and Jim finally walked away in disgust.

Just like the ongoing argument about separate dishes for each vegetable in a boiled dinner, this important matter about hanging clothes also has not been resolved—and never will be. However, my lines of clothes continue to present a well organized, neat appearance—and that is extremely important. (Note to Dell: Since you always side with Jim, I do not want your opinion on the proper way to hang clothes.)

However, Jim is far better than another husband I know. This fellow resided "out East" all of his life before moving to Soudan, and he refuses to let his wife hang clothes outside at all. In his neighborhood "out East," clothes lines were not permitted and clothes hanging on lines in other neighborhoods were signs of poverty. "Like they could not afford a clothes dryer," he explained. Each time I see my clothes on the outside line, with the wind choreographing their graceful, synchronized dances, I feel sorry for that man's wife. I cannot explain the intense feeling of satisfaction one gets from seeing a sparkling clean wash hanging in an organized fashion, dancing in the breeze.

WEATHER

With the passing of time, we find inaccuracies in many of the well-known, carved-in-stone sayings. For instance, "We can do nothing about changing the weather." Of course, that is not true, and we all know it. There is much we can do to change the weather.

Do we need rain? Then, take action. Wash the car. Hang out a batch of clothes. Go on a picnic. Go boating, golfing, fishing or to an outdoor celebration. Thoroughly water the garden. How about an outdoor wedding? Wash the outer side of the windows. Attend a baseball game. Air the bedding.

Would you prefer warmer temperatures? No problem. Put an extra blanket on the bed. Store the lightweight clothes. Install the storm windows. Go out pheasant hunting—in season, of course.

Or, maybe you want it cooler. Just reverse the above process, and go out fishing instead of hunting.

It is winter and you worried about the lack of insulating snow cover on your water and sewer lines. It is almost guaranteed—start out to keep that out-of-town appointment that took you two or three months to get, and the roads will be covered with a couple of feet of snow before you drive twenty miles.

It could get a little complicated, of course, if you decide that you want warmer weather and your neighbor is opting for cooler temperatures. Then it just boils down to which of you works the harder to effect the change.

ROMANS 10:12—*For there is no difference between the Jew and the Greek; for the same Lord over all is rich unto all that call upon him.*

Chapter 32

I am prone to developing an unhealthy attachment to "things"—household appliances, cars, favorite items of clothing, knick-knacks—everything! I admit that I am overly sentimental and entirely too emotional. Ironically, I am married to a man who is practical and matter-of-fact. He can sit through a funeral or a wedding and show no emotion. Give him credit, though. For all occasions, he always brings an ample supply of his handkerchiefs, which he unobtrusively passes to me when the need arises—and which I return to him, sodden and mascara-stained. He does pocket these wet, soggy handkerchiefs with a sigh and a look of disdain—but he endures. I am into lifetime commitments, without any reservations. One buys a car; it has to last forever. One buys a bathrobe; it is for life. Jim has no sentimentality and can shed possessions (or people, when necessary!) and get on with his life, with a philosophic, optimistic view. He, without a trace of guilt (and sometimes I detect even a hint of anticipation) can unabashedly refer to his "next wife" who will be a paragon of wifehood (if that was not a word, it is now!) She will possess all of the good qualities I lack and have no faults. He can trade in a faithful dependable car for a newer model, while I cling, sobbing, to the steering wheel, take countless pictures of the vehicle and watch in sorrow as he drives the old car away for the last time, happily trading it in for something new. He can toss greeting cards (with beautiful, touching messages!) into the trash.

Need I go on? You get the picture, and I am digressing a great deal. I have always had a great, warm relationship with my faithful clothes washer. For twenty-two years, we have been together. It has been loyal, trustworthy, never-failing and dependable. We relate! However, lately, my washer has been ailing. It was not a constant, ongoing illness, but rather an occasional recurring problem. One might describe it as a chronic illness. It was annoying to me, but after twenty-two years, one has to accept some tiny faults. Right? The first time it flooded the floor with water, I patiently wiped up the water, gave the washer a loving pat and told it that I hoped it would feel better. Tender, loving care can go a long way. The washer recovered from its temporary illness, and operated perfectly for a while. Another bout several weeks later was cause for more concern, but again it staged a remarkable recovery.

After the fourth incident, it became apparent even to me (Jim had made the determination after the first illness) that the washer needed help. I talked with a repair man, who said that what my appliance probably needed was a solenoid transplant. (I will admit that I had to call Bob Reichensperger to get the spelling.) The "organ" and the surgery would cost over one hundred dollars. "No way," said Jim. "We are not wasting that much money on a twenty-two-year-old machine." "But it is such a good machine," I argued tearfully. "It is almost like new!" I will not bore you readers with a detailed account of the conversation, which continued intermittently for several days. Suffice to say, we went shopping for a new washer, encountering severe cases of sticker shock, which I thought might get Jim to seeing my side of the situation. Not so! With a total lack of sensitivity, he would compare the attributes of the washers on display with the features of our present machine, seemingly totally unaware that "newer is not always better," and that he was doing a disservice to our dutiful, faithful washer waiting for us at home.

I returned home to my patient washer, sitting there, waiting to diligently wash our clothes, as it had done for years and years. "Maybe we should just buy the solenoid," I suggested, "maybe we should cancel the order for a new washer." In response, Jim started coldheartedly murdering the hapless machine. He wanted to see what controlled all of its complicated operations! It was heartbreaking to witness, and even Jim admitted that, all in all, the machine looked very healthy. Then he got down to some other diseased parts which were not affecting its present operation, but would be causing acute illnesses in the future.

I will make this long diatribe short. Our new machine is in, and my faithful machine, stripped down to a shell, sat outside for over a week. I could scarcely walk by it, I felt so guilty. So that is how it was rewarded for its years and years of service. I almost felt that I should explain to it that it was not my fault—the decision was Jim's—but that was not entirely true, because I did go along with the purchase of the new washer.

I have no emotional attachment to the new machine. Admittedly, it is doing a wonderful job of washing our clothes, but it seems smug, arrogant and entirely too self-satisfied. Almost as it were trying to show up the other machine! I am sure that we will begin to relate after ten or twelve years, although I am determined not to establish any emotional ties whatsoever with the new machine. My heart can be broken only so often.

PSALMS 33:20–22—*Our soul waiteth for the Lord; he is our help and our shield. For our heart shall rejoice in him, because we have trusted in his holy name. Let thy mercy, O Lord, be upon us, according as we hope in thee.*

Chapter 33

You respond to a knock on your door and open it to admit this perky, diminutive blonde, grasping a white paper bag. With sparkling blue eyes and a big, warm smile, she intones, "Avon Calling." It is a phrase she has repeated tens of thousands of times.

Eileen Swanson has been Tower's Avon Lady for over thirty-one years. She has been recognized for her outstanding salesmanship (The President's Club) and her years of service.

When Eileen began her Avon career, the firm focused on cosmetics. It soon expanded to include a line of jewelry and in the intervening years, it has become a woman's dream—a "portable" department store, offering clothing, handbags, books, adult and children's movies, toys, stuffed animals, home decorations for every holiday, even mosquito repellent, to list just a few. Eileen takes her Avon career very seriously, and the schedule in the Swanson home revolves around her orders and deliveries. Her husband, Lew, is well tuned to the dates of the arrival of her shipments, the dates her orders must be mailed and the days Eileen "delivers." Now that he is retired, he good-naturedly acts as chauffeur much of the time as she travels her routes.

Eileen also is active in her community and in her church and almost any event finds her bustling around the church kitchen or the Civic Center kitchen, serving on a "committee." She is forever "furnishing" for this or that event. A doting, indulgent grandmother, Eileen's three granddaughters are well aware that Grandma Eileen is a "soft touch." She will whip up a meal of eggs and bacon at any time of the day if one of the granddaughters expresses a desire for it. She enjoys cooking and especially loves to cook for her granddaughters. She always seems to know what they would like from her "catalogs," and she never disappoints them. Her youngest granddaughter lives in Illinois, but Eileen and Lew keep in very close touch and share her life via telephone.

Eileen often indulgently whips up a batch of cookies with the help of her younger "Soudan granddaughter." The fact that the baking might take considerably longer with all that help does not in any way diminish her pleasure of baking with a granddaughter at her side.

Miss a game in which one of granddaughters participated? I think not! When her granddaughters entered sports, Eileen was right there in the bleachers, bursting with pride, eyes sparkling, cheering them on! With a great deal of restraint and an equal amount of diplomacy, she would point out her granddaughter on the team and then bask in the praise of the granddaughter's performance. She never misses any type of performance of her two "girls," while regretting that she cannot be there to cheer on the third granddaughter.

Grandma Eileen's door is always open to the granddaughters. They can call at any time of the day and on any day of the week, asking if it would all right to come to visit. The answer is always in the affirmative. If Grandma Eileen is busy with her Avon orders, she just enlists the aid of her visiting granddaughter in getting the work done. (When they were younger, the "assistance" might have prolonged Grandma's task, but she was delighted to have her visitor.) She keeps goodies on hand for just such occasions.

When the granddaughters were younger, very, very few items of clothing in Grandma Eileen's closet and just a selected few cosmetics were "off limits" when they were playing "dress up." She had as much fun as the girls when they were parading around in her clothes.

Eileen keeps abreast of the news of all family members and is dismayed and concerned when one of them is ill or has a problem. "She really cares too much, but we appreciate her always keeping us in her thoughts and being there for us," said one of the family.

So, our Avon Lady has an active life, but her career remains one of her main focuses. She is an excellent representative for Avon. Years of experience have taught her what products her customers use, and she keeps a small supply of various items on hand, in case they "run out." "I just happen to have one on hand," she smiles, "so I can deliver it right away" -- and she does. She tactfully points out a new item which is becoming available and mentions merchandise which is selling at a special low price. Avon Calling!

2 CORINTHIANS 7:16—*I rejoice, therefore, that I have confidence in you in all things.*

Chapter 34

I tried to find the proper word to describe my feelings. Was it shock? No, that had come earlier. Was it, perhaps, grief? No, to me, grief can only be connected with death, or a tragic circumstance. Well, how about that good old "sentimental nostalgia?" There, too, the phrase seemed inadequate—descriptive of a more shallow emotion than I was experiencing. Could it be sympathy? Hardly—sympathy would seem to indicate that I was not directly involved, and I sincerely felt that I was.

I stood there as the wind began to whip the falling snow into angry, blizzard-like flurries. It seemed only a matter of minutes before the storm had erased the entire surroundings, and I was standing in an isolated spot, apart from the rest of the world. It all had an unreal atmosphere about it. I closely watched the faces of the men standing with me. Despite their attempts to mask their feelings, I sensed that they, too, were overcome with emotions they were unable to describe.

They continued their joking, much as they had for years, but their efforts seemed a little forced—or was it my imagination? A familiar odor permeated the air, and I was taken back in time to my childhood days. I had stood on that very same spot so many times in my youth. The lunch pails now held by the men brought back further memories. I remembered the terror that had come over me each time the earth seemed to rumble and threaten to collapse, plunging us down into its mysterious, dark depths. We had been cautioned against venturing too close, but the warnings were really not necessary. Only the menacing open pit on the opposite side kept us from standing back farther, and we stood rigid between the two terrors, inhaling the undefinable odor of what I always termed the "iron ore smell," which arose from the shaft.

Something was missing today, though, and I suddenly remembered the nauseating smell of the carbide lamps. Today's miners wore battery-powered lights, much brighter and certainly more reliable. As I had trembled there in fear, and yet in fascination, so many years ago, holding the lunch pail which was being sent to one of the miners, I was too young to begin to comprehend the magnitude of such a marvelous wonder as an underground iron ore mine. Last Friday, as I again stood on the same spot, my childish fears of those unknown, mystifying underground workings were mixed with a more adult appreciation of the marvels and excitement of underground mining.

The men standing with me were entering the mine for their last time. For most of them, the only way of life they had ever known was coming to an end. There is a relationship between the workers at the Soudan Mine that I doubt would be found anywhere else in the world. Some mysterious tie seems to bind them together, and while they do not intend to exclude the rest of the world, you somehow get the feeling that while they graciously welcome you into their midst you are still somewhat of an onlooker. They have their own private jokes—some passed down from generation to generation, repeated thousands of times. They recall pranks which have been played upon fellow workers—some of which have become almost legends, and which, by now, must certainly have grown rather exaggerated with their repeated relating.

I have always been of the opinion that when a man began his first day of work at the mine, there was an impressive ceremony, in which he received a new name, and from that day on he was known by no other title at the mine. Seldom are the names even words—most often, they seem to be syllables strung together. It is no exaggeration to say that, to their fellow workers the Christian name of some of the men is completely unknown, obscured by the many years of using his nickname. It is the absolute truth that men who have grown up in Soudan together and have worked together for, perhaps, twenty-five, thirty or even forty years, do not know each other's proper name.

Last Friday, as I stood with the men, there was the usual bantering. I detected, however, that some remarks brought tears to their eyes, no matter how hard they tried to suppress their real emotions. We found ourselves casting sidelong glances at the sturdy headframe which towered above us. Its appearance of powerful strength indicated a permanence which none of us felt at the moment. If I, who had never spent a day working in the mine, was choked with emotions, how must the men feel, having spent a greater part of their lives going through the same motions they were enacting today for the last time?

Somehow, it seemed that after seventy-eight years, the end should not come quite like this. There should have been a ceremony, perhaps—a ritual of some kind—a noted orator delivering a eulogy. A band playing stirring music (in a minor key, to suit the occasion). Yet, there the men stood, waiting for the cage, exactly as men had done for decades. The only difference today was the varied expressions on their faces—ranging from attempted joviality to graveness.

I could endure it no longer, and hastened to the engine house, whose interior, with its gigantic masses of steel and cables, only magnified my depression. Here, too, the gargantuan proportions of the machinery indicated ceaseless, enduring, perpetual—yes, eternal—operation. Here, too, I had stood as a child, watching, appalled, as the indicator pointed to the level in the mine at which the cage was suspended. My stay at the engine house was brief, and as the last men were raised in the cage, completing their final shift, and the cage returned to the earth, carrying more men down to begin their last day of work, I started for the car. As I passed the "dry," I heard the unbelievable sound of singing, as one of the miners, for the last time, washed away the red iron ore dust in the showers before changing to his street clothes.

As so many of the men had said, "It was unbelievable." Even as it was happening, the occasion had an almost dream-like quality. There was an air of finality, however, as the miners trudged through the whirling snow to their cars, lunch pails in hand, and carrying arm-loads of mining clothing which they would need no more.

REVELATION 22:21—*The grace of our Lord Jesus Christ be with you all. Amen.*

Chapter 35

I never could remember the correct advice. Does one "feed a fever and starve a cold," or "feed a cold and starve a fever?" Then, too, it becomes complicated if one has a cold AND a fever. I was collapsed on the sofa the other evening, surrounded by mountains of soggy Kleenex, and wrapped in my ragged, torn robe. (There is nothing like an old robe to make one feel comforted when ill.) My nose was red, my eyes were watering and my lips were cracked. I was listlessly watching television, since I was determined to die bravely and heroically.

Flashed upon the television screen was a picture of a young woman in a filmy negligee, her hair beautifully done. From the slight frown on her beautiful face, one knew that something was awry in the gorgeous woman's life, and soon it was revealed. Her husband arrived home, all sympathy and solicitude. It seems that the problem was that the woman has a cold. He gives her a cold tablet, the concern on his face giving the viewer the idea that he considers this cold somewhat of a tragedy, comparable to the earthquake in Managua.

Time flies by on television at an even faster rate than in reality, and the very next second we are transported in time to the following day. Here is the wife, flitting gaily around the house, acting idiotically happy. The husband arrives home, and she greets him as if he were returning from an African safari. It develops that she has shampooed the rugs, scrubbed all the walls, taken excellent care of their twenty children, entertained fifty women at bridge and is raring to go out for an evening of fun.

I sat there, hair standing on end, looking like a reject from the morgue, and I would have given anything to ruin that perfect coiffure and wipe that stupid, giddy grin from her face.

My husband chose this moment to come into the room. "Good gosh, you look terrible," he says. "If you're trying out for the role of Rudolph, The Red-Nosed Reindeer, you're a little late, as usual," he adds. I try to gather together enough strength to flash him a look of hatred, but my feeble efforts must have been in vain, because he continued, "Do you think you're going to make it?" The question carried a great deal more curiosity than concern, I thought.

Now, I'll flash to the next day at our house. You don't find me acting like Pollyanna. No sir! In fact, the scene hasn't changed much from the previous day, except that my nose is redder, my head is stuffier, and I am about fifty times more irritable. When the husband walks into this scene, I have scarcely more than a muffled greeting for him. "How do you feel?" he asks absentmindedly, as he settles down to watch television. "I think I am dying," I gasp. Already engrossed in his program, he mutters, "That's good. How anyone can look like death warmed over one day and still survive for another day is beyond me."

Do you want to know the irony of the whole thing? I took the very same pills as the woman in the television commercial. I think that I am going to sue!

GALATIANS 3:26—*For ye are all the children of God by faith in Christ Jesus.*

Chapter 36

I watched our daughter cross the street and, chattering nervously with her friends, start out for her first day of junior high school. For several weeks she had been conditioning us to the transition from grade school to junior high, and I noted with another pang that her absurdedly long, skinny legs, tanned by the summer sun, were concealed under the required skirts of a teenager. The fact that she had often, in the past weeks, expressed a genuine reluctance to "grow up" made her new role more heartbreaking than ever.

With envy, I saw the next-door neighbor taking movies of her young son, starting out for his very first day at school. Wasn't it only yesterday that our dear child had entered kindergarten? We, too, had taken pictures to record the important event, and I remember thinking that never again would I know such heartbreak. I smiled wryly through my tears as I realized that I, too, had done a lot of growing up in the years following that first day of school, when I had left my little girl in kindergarten and started home without her.

It has often been said that the admission of a shortcoming is half the battle; in my case, it just is not true. One of my most annoying faults is my desire to cherish too dearly and too closely those whom I love. Each milestone in our daughter's rapid development has brought not only pride, but pain. Her first steps thrilled me, yet, even then, I realized how fast time flies, and how soon children grow up.

There is nothing in the world as wonderful as raising a child. From her first smile, we have watched her every action with obvious delight and wonder. She is truly not a spoiled girl; we have disciplined her more than is absolutely necessary. I will never cease to be amazed, however, at the sweet, thoughtful, unusual ways which make me marvel. Admittedly, we are prejudiced, but the fact that she is, indeed, a most wonderful girl is evidenced by the many stories of her deeds which are circulated and repeated throughout our small town.

Yes, we've watched her grow up. Her first day at school, chicken pox, measles, stitches in her head from being hit with a baseball bat, the nights of anxiety when she was ill, her first year at Bible camp, her first bus ride alone, her broken arm, the terror at seeing her beautiful face torn and bleeding from a dog bite. The countless joys, the countless sorrows, some times of disappointment, of course, when she just couldn't quite come up to the too high standards we had set for her. We have grown up, too. Her complete delight and pleasure with life and all it holds, her intense interest in everything in the world, and her belief that it was all put there just for her to enjoy, couldn't help but change our outlooks to some degree, too.

Her reluctance to grow up is shown in so many heartbreaking little ways. Rough-housing with her father, playing wildly with her big dog, running, jumping, slamming doors. In many ways, she is still our little girl. Then I watch her walk sedately up the street, I see her calmly handle a difficult situation with the ease of an adult, I watch her stand before the mirror and fuss with her hair. Then I know that in such a very short time our little girl will be a young lady.

No longer do I view each milestone as the most heartbreaking moment of my life. I know now that we will go on to greater heartaches. Her first day at school was nothing compared to watching her walk off to a new junior high school today. As she grows up and leaves us, there will be more pangs. High school, graduation, college, her first job, and marriage. God-willing, we will suffer with her through the agonies of childbirth—and then the unsurpassed joys and sorrows of raising her own children. As they say, that's life, and you can't beat living—especially when you're living with our daughter!

HEBREWS 12:14—*Follow peace with all men, and holiness, without which no man shall see the Lord.*

Chapter 37

Well, this is the season for red-rimmed eyes, sniffles and difficulty in breathing—and I don't mean colds! While others are busy Christmas shopping, mailing cards, decorating, baking, etc., I spend my time hauling cases of Kleenex home from the store—and then using their contents.

For me, the "Christmas feeling" is one emotion-filled time after another. I'm certainly not bragging, believe me. I wish I could be different. I wouldn't care so much if I could control my emotions to the extent of an appealing tear coursing delicately down my cheek. But that's not for me! My face twists all up in an effort to control my tears, and then I slobber and sob uncontrollably.

What tragedies bring on these emotional outbursts? Well, someone wishing me a "Merry Christmas," watching a youngster out Christmas shopping, seeing a plate of beautiful Christmas cookies displayed on the television screen or just thinking about the holiday season.

I cry in lonesomeness for my loved ones who aren't home for Christmas. I cry in sorrow for my loved ones who are no longer with us at all. I cry for those whom I know who are experiencing sorrow and loneliness. Well, I cry for happy things, too.

A card and note from our niece, in which she reminisces about the past, sent me into a torrential downpour of tears. Not satisfied, I read the note again the next day, with the same dampening effect.

I attended the Christmas vocal concert of the Tower grades, and wore dark glasses and kept my head lowered to avoid looking like an absolute fool, sitting there crying. (My friend??, Hal Ayers, would be happy to tell you that those procedures don't help at all in making me look like less of a fool.)

I choke up looking at the Christmas decorations which have survived all these years in our home. (Their survival can be attributed, for the most part, to the fact that they never get put up!) Remembering our daughter's joy over some of the decorations when she was a little girl, I collapse into convulsive sobbing.

The Sunday School Christmas program, with those dear, innocent children telling the wonderful Christmas story—and the beautiful story itself—are further cause for tears. The Christmas cantata of the high school and freshmen chorus added a deeper hue of red to my nose and my eyes. And the Christmas carolers on Main Street on Wednesday just absolutely broke me up. The music was beautiful and clear!

Well, you are all busy with your Christmas preparations, so I won't bore you with further details. I'll save the rest for my psychiatrist.

I do take some time out to get angry, too. For instance, when a whole week before Christmas there is an ad for "Last Minute Shopping!" Last-minute shopping is on Christmas Eve, or the day after Christmas. How ridiculous can they get, using that term before the Christmas season is even upon us?

Would you like to hear that I am improving in my Christmas un-preparations? Would you like to have me tell you that my cards are sent, my gifts are purchased and wrapped, my baking is done, my home is decorated? I'd like to be able to tell you those things, too—but I am a very poor liar.

So—sob, sob, sniffle, sniffle—a Merry Christmas to each one of you. I do mean this with all my heart. You readers are very dear to me and I sincerely want happiness, health and success for each of you. You are truly the greatest people ever. We need your encouragement and assistance, believe me! And you continue to give those things to us in full measure.

May the coming year hold many happy times for you.

LUKE 2:11—*For unto you is born this day, in the city of David, a Savior, which is Christ the Lord.*

Chapter 38

Fire Chief Jim Moraski stopped into the office on Tuesday afternoon. The members of the area Fire Departments were completing their special schooling in fire fighting and search-and-rescue. The "final examination" would be that evening, when the home of the late Louis Schrader would be burned down, and the firemen would use all the procedures they had been studying.

Yes, I assured the fire chief, my husband, Jim, would want to be there to take pictures. "You better come along, too," he urged. "You can get a lot of information on the course from the instructor, Don McKay." And that is how I happened to be accompanying Jim when he went to take pictures.

I met the personable Mr. McKay. He was unbelievably busy, organizing the members of the various fire departments and setting the scene for the fire. He patiently took time to give me some details, and introduced me to "Woody" Walters. Both men are state fire training field instructors.

At one point in the conversation, Mr. McKay informed me that the only way to really get an idea of fire fighting was to be on the scene—right in the burning building. I thought that was a sensible idea, all right, and I decided that I would talk with the first group of firemen after they had completed their stint of the fire fighting, and get their "on-the-spot" reaction. I was totally unprepared for his next statement—a suggestion that I accompany the firemen when they entered the burning building. He assured me that I would be in no danger, because he or "Woody" would watch out for me. I'm not saying that I ever consented—I'm not saying that I DIDN'T.

The next thing I knew, he was handing me a fireman's coat. Noting my complete confusion (not to mention utter panic!) a young lady from Crane Lake, Katy Klaysmat, showed me how the coat must be fastened. A helmet, boots, gloves and air mask were provided.

Believe me, I'll never be a woman's libber. I'm all for chivalry—there can't be too much of it! With comments from Jim on the rapid decline of my mentality, I gratefully and willingly accepted the assistance of the firemen, who helped me on with the big, clumsy boots, placed the air tank (or whatever it is!) on my back, fastened the helmet on my head, and, to my horror, clamped the face mask on my face. I wouldn't have been heard if I had screamed for help, and I knew that the first indication they would have that I wasn't getting air was when I collapsed in a heap on the ground. I was positive that I couldn't even rip the mask from my face, because it was strapped on so well.

Mr. McKay assembled the firemen for their final instructions. He carefully reviewed the entire procedure, explaining in detail how each situation was to be handled, and what fire fighting technique was to be used. He or "Woody" would be with the fire fighters inside the building at all times. "This is a real fire. You are faced with real danger. There is always the possibility of injury—this is for real!" I'm not quoting him exactly, but that was the message he conveyed to the firemen—and to me!

As the first group of fire fighters approached the building, Mr. McKay motioned for me to join them. I don't know if it was the heavy boots or heavier air tank that held me to the spot where I was standing—I'd like to think that was the case. However, I finally realized what I had consented to do. I moved woodenly along, and was helped into the building. Taking a firm grasp of my hand, Mr. McKay moved me along with the fire fighters, and we approached the door beyond which the fire was raging. "Get down," he shouted to me as the door was swung open, and we were confronted with a wall of flames. The firemen went into action, orders were shouted, and I was dazedly aware of a lot of motion around me. "Move back," he commanded, and I started to arise. "Get down," he shouted, and I rapidly fell to my knees, as I watched the flames. "Are you all right?" he asked, and I answered that I was, but, of course, he couldn't hear me. He never relinquished his tight grip on my hand—or was it I who was clutching his hand?

Suddenly, the flames were gone, and we were enveloped in darkness. In terror, I looked towards where I thought the outside door should be, and was confronted with blackness. Mr. McKay released his grip on my hand. "You take over, Woody," he shouted and another hand grasped me firmly, "Woody," too, inquired about my well-being. I watched in fascination as a burning ember fell near my feet. I was comforting myself with Mr. McKay's earlier statement that they wouldn't let anything happen to me. Then I remembered "Woody's" statistic that a fire fighter dies on duty every three days. I wasn't fighting any fire—in fact, I had all I could do to fight the terror I was experiencing.

I now sensed rather than saw the action around me. Orders continued to be shouted, but blackness hung heavily about us. (I later learned it was smoke.) I have since reflected that it was the raging fire which presented the actual danger, but the moment when I felt the most terror—the time when I suddenly realized the extent of my foolish action which placed me in such a predicament—was when the flames were temporarily brought under control and we were plunged into thick darkness. I had been at least a little prepared for fire—but not for being suddenly trapped in that awful black void.

Mercifully, the men decided that I had had sufficient experience— actually, I think they felt that I had been in the way long enough. I was escorted from the burning building, and with a prayer of thanks, I stumbled into daylight.

Mr. McKay is right. Until one has had the terrifying experience, there is no way to understand what a fire fighter goes through. No human being should be exposed to such danger and terror. I'm sure that listening to lectures for hundreds of hours, reading every book written on the subject and discussing the situation with other firemen still leaves an inexperienced fireman unprepared for such action. Mr. McKay had warned the firemen in his final instructions that they would tend to panic, no matter how much they felt in control of the situation while they were still outside.

I really had been safe inside. I had someone watching out for me. I was not right in there fighting the blaze. Those firemen were. I've always had a great deal of respect for firemen, but after my experience, I feel they have to be super-human to go through what they do.

Mr. McKay had warned me that it wouldn't be anything like what I had seen on television programs. He was so right!

I've never been of the opinion that anything men can do, women can do better. I've always felt that there were some fields in which women had no business. Fire fighting, definitely, is one of them. Hats off (helmets, air tanks and air masks, too!) to the firemen. They have my respect—they are special people. This was a planned, organized practice session. I can't even imagine the terror of an actual fire fighting situation.

I'll tell you one thing. I'm throwing away my equal rights button. (My husband would never let me wear it, anyway!)

2 THESSALONIANS 3:1—*Finally, brethren, pray for us, that the word of the Lord may have free course, and be glorified, even as it is with you.*

Chapter 39

This is not necessarily based on personal experience. (I've been threatened about writing about You-Know-Who!) What is that phrase? "It does not necessarily refer to real characters or to actual events. Any reference to any person, living or dead, is a coincidence." The scene is a husband and wife, out partridge hunting in the woods. I call it "Progression of a Marriage."

First Year—"Here, doll, let me carry you over the puddle. I don't want you to get your feet wet."

Second Year—"Give me your hand, darling, and I'll help you across the ditch."

Third Year—"I'll hold this branch back, dear. Hurry along."

Tenth Year—"Did the branch hurt you? Well, you should know better, woman. Only a dummy would follow that closely going through this brush."

Fifteenth Year—"For gosh sakes, can't you be quiet? You sound like an elephant coming through the woods. You've scared away every partridge within ten miles."

Twentieth Year—"Would you move over or else go sit in the back? You're crowding the poor dog." (This is traveling by car, en route to the hunting area.)

Twenty-fifth Year—"Are you coming along back there? You can't just shuffle your feet, woman, you have to move along. Hurry up and catch up or stay home next time."

There is no twenty-sixth year. After that, the woman can be found sitting in her rocking chair, waiting for her husband to come home from hunting.

MATTHEW 6:14—*But if ye forgive not men their trespasses, neither will your Father forgive your trespasses.*

Chapter 40

On many occasions during the past fourteen and one-half years, I have written about the antics of our black Labrador, Bucky. This is the final chapter in the life of Bucky Burgess. He left us on May 23. We called him Bucky, although his registered name was "Jim's Shadow," but by the time it would take to get all those syllables out, Bucky would have been a mile away when we called him. He was well aware of his registered name, however, and spent every minute of his life living up to it, usually so close to Jim's heels that Jim kept tripping over him.

The veterinarian's bill for services termed it "euthanasia." How like our society to affix a socially acceptable term to the most heinous of deeds—and not call a spade a spade. We had hoped and prayed that Bucky would make it easy for us. His health had deteriorated tragically in the past eighteen months. In fact, it was over two years ago that Jim constructed a ramp to make it easier for poor old Bucky to get up and down from the deck. As the veterinarian said, "He just won't give up." He sensed that we just could not live without him, and he was going to be there for us, no matter how difficult life was for him. We made—and broke—several "appointments" during the couple of weeks before he died, unable to take that impossible last step and hoping that Bucky could "go in his sleep." It was not to be.

The night before the final "appointment," our dear young friend, Alan, came down to be with us, to say good-bye and to bring Bucky's girlfriend, Brandy. Brandy and Bucky greeted each other with their customary kiss, but Brandy seemed uneasy and edgy and was relieved when Alan let her outside. It was really eerie how she sensed that something was terribly wrong.

Alan and Jim spent a couple of hours reminiscing about the many hunts in which Bucky had excelled. He was an incredible, remarkable hunter, with unrestrained enthusiasm, unlimited determination and energy—and his usual attitude that the whole world had been created just for him. Before the hunters had even taken their guns from the car and had donned their hunting gear, Bucky would often have taken off into a field like a bullet and come back with a crippled pheasant. Now, this is not acceptable behavior for a hunting dog, and even though he would settle down after a short time and set about to hunt more seriously and sanely, he thought of hunting as a delightful, challenging experience for HIM—the hunters, he allowed, certainly could do their own thing.

So, to direct all that unbridled enthusiasm and uncanny ability into the proper channels, Bucky was sent to a trainer. I died a little as we left him at the kennels. I had admired Bucky's spirit and zest for life and did not want him "tamed." We were told that to make this training successful, we were not to come to visit Bucky. That did not mean that we could not call, and we kept the telephone lines busy. It seemed that this trainer, who could boast of a number of international field champions, was having trouble with our Bucky. "He is the most stubborn dog I have ever had," the trainer said in exasperation. "Way to go!" was the message I mentally sent to Bucky over the miles. "He has a mind of his own," the trainer observed. Well, of course, he did! Bucky considered himself a step above mere humans—and in many ways he was superior.

The training period kept getting extended week after week, until we finally got the word—Bucky was making progress! Would we mind if Bucky were one of the dogs the trainer took to Missouri? I minded very much—Jim thought it would be a good experience. Bucky went. Eventually, after what seemed like several lifetimes, a subdued Bucky returned to us, maybe not graduating summa cum laude, but at least graduating.

I set about to make up for all the indignity and hardship he had gone through, with Jim arguing that I was undoing all the benefits of that dreadful training experience. We came to a workable solution and Bucky began to exhibit a little more restraint in his hunting. He was an outstanding, indefatigable hunter, notwithstanding the fact that he continued to delight in plunging into a field and clearing it of pheasants in record time. We have other fields to conquer; let us get on with this. He was a dynamo, crashing through—not over—windfalls, plunging into barbed wire fences, emerging cut and bleeding by the end of a hunt. After a few practice runs at the onset of each hunt, he would settle down to serious, methodical hunting, and he was spectacular to watch. He would near a spot where he had flushed a partridge two or three years earlier, moving tensely and cautiously. He remembered every one of the hundreds of spots where he had flushed a bird.

Jim and Alan sat there that painfully sad night before "the appointment," recalling all those happy times and reviewing many of Bucky's uncanny retrieves, with Alan occasionally reaching down to ruffle Bucky's fur. Bucky's tail would wag and he would reach up to give Alan a kiss.

His last two years were not quality time for poor old Buck. He got so crippled that he could not get up by himself, and we would have to support his back end to get him on his feet. In all the years we had him, he had come upstairs at my heels each night when I went to bed, and lie by the bed where I could reach out and pet him or touch him with my foot. It became painful for him to negotiate the stairs, and sometimes he would stumble, but he determinedly continued the practice until, finally, after he had fallen down the stairs a couple of times, he opted to remain downstairs at night. It broke my heart to ascend those stairs every night as he watched me from the sofa—helpless and abandoned. For a number of months near the end, he could no longer manage to get up on the sofa, and he would watch from a vantage point on the floor.

Gradually, his back legs began to fail, and he would often stagger as he walked. Then his back legs began to scarcely function at all, and Nancy Yapel sewed lovely slings, with sherpa lining and handles, so we could support his back end as he walked. Sometimes he staggered along, sometimes he just dragged his back legs, but he kept going and I prayed for a miracle. One day, after several months, Bucky got up by himself and walked across the room! That was the only time he was able to get up by himself, but for the next couple of months he began to walk again, however haltingly, and we were overjoyed.

Our happiness was short-lived, and when Bucky's legs ceased to function the next time, he went downhill rapidly. He could scarcely get up and down the ramp, even with our support, and when he reached the bottom, he would collapse with exhaustion. Towards the end, he would stand at the bottom of the ramp, looking up at the short slope, panting and exhausted. "I don't think I can make it," he would say, and we would encourage him, letting him stop to rest along the way.

In spite of his illness, he remained a beautiful, gorgeous dog until the very end. His coat shone a lustrous black, he was alert and attentive, and lying down, he looked like a young, spirited animal. He never lost his control over us, and since he could not get up and walk, he would "woof" his orders. He could no longer emit those deafening barks with which he controlled us all those years, but his muffled woofs were just as effective. If his meal was five minutes late, he would woof reproachfully. "My meal. My Meal. I want my meals on time. You are late and I am starving." I would bustle around, hurriedly getting his food, his medication and his water, while he impatiently continued to woof.

"How do you get Bucky to take all his pills?" people would ask. The intelligence of this incredible dog knew no bounds. I would take the pill, put it by his mouth and gently open his lips. He would immediately open his mouth so I could force the pill down his throat. After months of this practice, I felt that it was too hard on Bucky's throat to keep administering all those pills that way, so I would put the medication in soft bread and he would gobble the pills down hungrily. His appetite never waned.

People would not believe the intelligence of this dog. When he was injured and had to have a bandage or dressing changed, he would see us coming with the bandages and would roll over, holding up the injured paw or exposing his wounded tummy so we could treat him. During the last months of his life, I used treated "wipes" to give him a "bath" a couple of times a day. He would see me coming with the "wipes," roll over on his side, close his eyes and relax while I bathed him, a treatment which always soothed and calmed him.

In my haste to satisfy his every wish and avoid his displeasure, I would sometimes place his water dish in front of him without refilling it with fresh water. "Stale water?" he would sniff in disgust, as he pushed the dish away. "I want fresh water—NOW," he would woof. This is the same dog that would drink thirstily from a mud puddle when he was out hunting, but absolutely refused water treated with softener, shunning anything but spring water—fresh, if you please—when he was at home.

There is no way that the life of our amazing Bucky can be capsulated into one article. It would take a whole book to recount his antics. We are inconsolable, absolutely devastated, over his death. He was a special, remarkable dog—and we are glad that we were his! There never was, and never will be, another Bucky! He left a void impossible to fill. Our lives are empty without him, and our tiny home has suddenly become cavernous. We now know the full meaning of "deadly silence."

A more loyal, faithful, eager-to-please partner could never be found. He spent his entire life trying to do exactly what we wanted of him—always looking up at us to see if his actions met our approval. He reveled in our praise. We expected too much of him—and always got more than we expected or deserved.

MATTHEW 11:28—*Come unto me, all ye that labour and are heavy laden, and I will give you rest.*

Chapter 41

My nephew, brother-in-law, and I were going into the garage. We opened the overhead garage door using a truly ingenious device which Jim had "invented." We turned on the lights with an elaborate pulley system which Jim had rigged up. My nephew knelt down to look at Jim's ATV, and he looked up, smiling broadly through tear-filled eyes. "That Uncle Jim!" was all he said. All three of us knew exactly what he meant. In less than a minute, we had viewed three of the thousands of innovative, clever devices Jim had fashioned to solve a problem or make an "improvement" on his property. When his legs no longer were strong enough to shift the ATV, he made a hand shift so he could continue to ride his machine. My nephew, extremely mechanically inclined, realized just how ingenious Jim's "inventions" were.

My active husband was always "fixing things" or creating some new device. Thousands of times I came home from work to find him at his work bench in the garage, even times when it was much too cold for him to be outside.

Often as I approached, he would say, "You came just in time. I need some help here." You can be certain it was not technical advice he wanted. He had dropped a screw, a bolt, a spring or some such thing on the floor and could not find it. "Here is what you are looking for," he would explain, showing me a mate to the missing piece. Or he would want me to hold something steady so he could work on it. I honestly think that he was happy when something broke, so he could fix it. If there was nothing to repair (which, in our home was a rare occasion), he would decide that something needed improvement.

"Wouldn't it be easier for you if - - - " and he would explain what he intended to do to make some device "easier for me." I would insist that whatever he had singled out for his magic touch was just fine as it was, and he would explain what had to be done to "improve it." He ignored me, not even dignifying my protests with further explanation, and a couple of days later when I got home from work, he would excitedly say, "Now, try this and see if it is not much, much better." He was extremely clever, not only at repairs and improvements, but also at getting his own way.

The first of Jim's rules as he tackled a repair, improvement or maintenance job was to go through his "supplies." He never, ever bought anything if he could scrounge it from his vast stores of pipes, screws, lumber, nails, pieces of metal, bolts, etc. When all else failed, he would make a trip to the solid waste collection site, usually returning with exactly what he needed, plus some other treasures that "somebody was foolish enough to throw away." If he could not find what he wanted, he would modify something to meet his requirements. It was a matter of principle with him, and I know he found as much pleasure in using materials he had on hand or that he could salvage as he did working on the task.

As he completed a repair, he would emphasize over and over that he had not had to buy a thing. It was not that he was penurious; using what was on hand was part of the challenge, and Jim enjoyed challenges. Our daughter affectionately called him "Salvage Sam" for many, many years. One cannot go more than a foot or two anywhere in our home, garage or out in our yard without encountering a creation or repair attributable to Jim and his ingenuity.

Even during his monthly visits to the dialysis center in Duluth, he would make suggestions about how their complicated, sophisticated, state-of-the-arts equipment could be improved. When he visited the next month, he was always annoyed that they had not followed up on his advice, especially when they had agreed with him that his ideas were excellent.

There were a few repairs that were not exactly perfect, but in our sixty years together, his record of achievement was nothing less than amazing. Years ago, our clothes washer would not open at the end of the "spin" cycle, and I really had to struggle with it to get the lid open. I do not remember exactly how I opened the lid each time, but when Jim found out I had been having trouble and had not mentioned it to him, he was disgusted and irritated. "Why didn't you tell me?" he fumed. "I can fix that." In a day or so he announced triumphantly that he had fixed the washer. "Come here and let me show you," he bragged. "Now, here is what you have to do. When you want to open the lid, you just take your fist and give the lid a good whack right here. Now watch, because you have to hit it in exactly the right place." Problem solved and the washer served us well for many more years, with me "whacking" it in just the right spot.

All his friends, as well as our family members, knew of Jim's endless stock of even the most unusual repair supplies, and they often came down to check with him when they needed just one or two of something for a job on which they were working. "I have just what you want," Jim would say and he would go directly to the item in question. This was the same man who could not find something in the cupboard which was right in plain sight! "Don't move things," he would grumble.

Seeing a neighbor working on a project piqued Jim's curiosity and interest, and he would rush over to see what the neighbor was doing. Often, he would hurry back home to get some tool or some piece of equipment and hurry back to "help." It made his day. If his assistance were not needed, he would stay to supervise the job, with

148

endless suggestions. He was never happier than when he was helping someone, and there seemed to be neighborhood projects to keep him happy when his own "To Do" list got shorter. He always had about twenty or thirty tasks on his "To Do" list, which he personally kept updated. I really do not remember even one time when I suggested a project to add to that endless list. He checked his list every morning and he referred to it as he planned his day. "I have to stay busy," he would explain.

He said thousands of times that he never once regretted retiring and that he enjoyed every single day of his retirement years. During the first years, of course, he devoted a great deal of his time to hunting, fishing, snowmobiling, building deer stands, clearing walking trails and anything else that would take him outdoors. He enjoyed twenty-six years of retirement and when his health declined and he was unable to do as much as he would have liked, he would stubbornly, determinedly keep going, struggling through countless difficulties. Even as he sat and looked out the window, on many occasions he would say, "Just to sit here and be able to look at the lake. I never tire of it. God is so good to me."

I realize that Jim was fortunate. How many people retire and never live to cash their first Social Security check? How many live only a few years after they retire? I know I should be more grateful for the many years he had, and I really do thank God, but I am greedy. Such a dynamic, complicated man, who made such an impact on so many lives. He really was not ready to leave us and we were certainly not prepared to accept his departure, but I guess God knew best. He is now up in Heaven, explaining to God how the "Heavenly Gates" can be improved. Jim had us all convinced that "Jim's way is best."

JOHN 14:27—*"Peace I leave with you, my peace I give unto you; not as the world giveth, give I unto you. Let not your heart be troubled, neither let it be afraid."*

Chapter 42

I am still riddled with guilt. I cannot believe that I did it, and I am so ashamed. It was one of our bitterly cold, windy days, when one just could not endure being outside for more than a few minutes, at the most. I was driving from Ely, and here was a woman hitchhiking. There had been no car pulled onto the shoulder of the road, so she had not had car trouble. I was so, so tempted to stop and give her a ride, but I callously drove on by, my conscience in overdrive. I thought of the story of the Good Samaritan in the Bible, and I almost turned around.

Then I thought of the co-worker of our neighbor, Ron, who did pick up a young couple on the road from Virginia to International Falls. They found his body in a field adjacent to the road after a search was initiated when he did not return home.

Then I cruised into my "It is not my fault" mode. What woman in her right mind would set out walking on a day like this? I became indignant, obviously in an attempt to lighten my guilt. Truly, though, who would do such a stupid thing? Then I thought of my brothers who, on more than one occasion, had hitchhiked home when they had a short military leave. They could not have come home were it not for the compassion of the motorists.

Jim always picked up all hitchhikers, taking them to their destinations, which often differed from his. Half way to Ely, to Embarrass, to the Vermilion Reservation. He could not, just could not, pass by anyone seeking a ride. Even the story of the murdered man did not deter him. I often sat in the car, terrified if the hitchhiker even moved a leg or an arm, expecting the cold barrel of a gun at my head at any moment.

Even now, I continue to waver: Should I have picked her up? Was it wiser to drive on by? I was grateful, as I read the newspapers more thoroughly than usual for a few days, to learn that no woman was found injured, suffering from frostbite, or worse. A better person than I had come along!

PROVERBS 16:20—*He that handleth a matter wisely shall find good; and whoso trusteth in the Lord, happy is he.*

Chapter 43

I am always amused by the terms people use to discreetly explain their status with the person with whom they live. Such "cutesy" expressions—significant other, partner, live-in, soul mate, life companion, loving companion, special friend, lifelong friend. Such imaginations!

I will be blunt, shunning whimsical terms for "just the fact." I no longer live alone. It was a matter of much discussion and some argument among the members of my family. My sister emphatically vetoed the idea. Her daughter, on the other hand, thought that it was a good way to "start looking forward," and even volunteered to introduce me to a couple of "prospects." Surprisingly, my daughter not only approved, but practically insisted that I take the step and she, too, volunteered to introduce me to a couple of "possibles." My nephew chose to take a "wait and see" attitude and repeatedly told me that I would know when I was ready to take such action, but he, too, offered "assistance" at the proper time. You see, in my family, everyone has input into any decision made in the family circle, especially one of this magnitude.

It took a great deal of prodding and a greater amount of pondering, but when the pressure to take action came at me from all sides—I made up my mind (to be truthful, family members more or less "kind of" took over the decision-making process). No more living alone! It was my nephew whom I approached with my decision, and he already had a "prospect" in mind. My sister and her husband have mellowed considerably and "kind of" now accept my decision, although they are still apprehensive about my "companion" treating me well.

A member of the church approached me several weeks ago. There is no such thing as a "secret" in Tower-Soudan. She chided me for not having informed her of my new status. How she found out, I will never know, unless it was divulged by the husband of another church member who had stopped in one day and had seen my "companion." I really have not been trying to hide the fact, but neither have I been broadcasting it from the rooftops.

My "companion" is beautiful—big, blue eyes, striped legs, face and tail, a gorgeous white chest and a "sparkly" grey back. Her name is Jasmine. My nephew, who works at an animal hospital in Virginia and volunteers at the Mesabi Humane Society, had been keeping an eye on Jasmine as a distinct "possible." He assured me that after introductions, if I did not like his choice for me, he would be happy to introduce me to others.

One huge deterrent was the fact that I am a "dog" person. I know absolutely nothing about felines and I love, love, love canines. A dog was discarded as a possibility because dogs have to be walked at night, even in forty degree below weather, even on lonely, rather isolated roads. "We would worry about your walking a dog at night, Mom," my daughter tried to reason with me. Now, a cat——

I would have imagined that the people at the Humane Society would be thrilled to lessen the number of cats they house. It did not seem that way to me. I was taken into an office and seated while they brought Jasmine in. I was told that if Jasmine took a dislike to me, I would have to look further. They would not force this poor little cat on someone whom she did not like. They armed me with bribes (cat treats, a brush to groom her), probably knowing that Jasmine would not accept me on my charm alone.

We spent a tense ten or fifteen minutes "selling" me to Jasmine and then she was returned to her cage and I was interviewed. Pages of questions to answer, and the situation again began to seem hopeless. "I swear to tell the truth and nothing but the truth, so help me God." Had I ever owned a cat before? (Has anyone ever <u>owned</u> a cat?) Was I familiar with the care of a cat? The list went on and on, and my answers were all negative. In preparation for this big step, my daughter and her husband had purchased a "Cat Manual" for me, and it certainly contained everything anyone would want to know about cats, but I had no "hands-on" experience. I seemed to sense a growing coolness towards me by the Humane Society staff. A grown woman who did not understand cats! A person working for the Humane Society would consider such a person uneducable. My nephew kept trying to smooth things over; he is so tactful and charming, so diplomatic.

I do not know if this is standard procedure, but I signed six or seven papers, swore to a number of conditions and paid the fee. However, I could not have the cat. She would be "delivered" by my nephew the following day, if "everything went right." What was that suppose to mean?

"What have I done?" I repeated over and over on the way home. "I cannot believe I did not weigh this decision more carefully," I mumbled. I slept very little that night.

My nephew arrived with my "live-in" the next evening. As a Mother's Day present, my daughter and her husband had paid for everything a cat could ever want or need—food, litter, litter box, bed, toys, brush, dishes. With instructions from my nephew, we got Jasmine settled—or as settled as she is ever going to be. The instructions that my nephew left for her care are more lengthy than those for making and launching a missile. I got the drift immediately when each instruction ended with the statement, "but if the cat does not seem to want you to (whatever) discontinue it immediately."

It now boils down to whether Jasmine will allow me to continue to live in the house. I try to obey all her orders and I do everything I can to make her happy, but sometimes I have no idea what "meow, meow, meow" means, and patience is not one of her virtues. My daughter informed me that cats reveal a great deal about their moods by the way they wag their tails. I have tried to analyze her "tail messages," but there is absolutely a serious lack of communication there! I realize that I am on very shaky ground, as far as my relationship with this cat!

PROVERBS 18:22—*Whoso findeth a wife findeth a good thing, and obtaineth favor from the Lord.*

Chapter 44

My cousin stopped at the office one day last week with a "treat" for me to enjoy with my tea. She also brought a present for Jasmine, my cat. The following day was my day off and as I went into the back room later in the morning I was confronted with a scene I will never forget. I never close the zipper on my purse and there was Jasmine plunged into the purse, with everything whirling out of it. Pens, notes, notebook, envelopes, my monthly check that I received the previous day, my coin purse (now devoid of coins), my checkbook. Some of the papers were torn, some had ragged teeth marks. I rushed over and grabbed Jasmine's collar, and she stopped in her frenzy long enough to try to bite me, and then went back to attempt to complete the disaster.

I was scared to death. Jasmine had gone berserk! I had heard of cat fever. Maybe that is what she had. I hurried upstairs for a blanket in which to capture her and get her to the animal hospital.

Suddenly another possibility dawned on me—Jasmine must have a mouse cornered in my purse. Now I had to figure out how to get Jasmine out of the purse and the purse outside so the mouse could escape.

Suddenly, Jasmine shot out of the back room with something in her mouth, and I rushed over for a closer inspection. It was then that I realized that my cousin's gift to Jasmine must be catnip.

I was telling my nephew about the incident, and I asked him how cats acted when they had cat fever. Very quietly, in a monotone, with no emphasis, he said, "People get cat fever, Aunt Phil. People get cat fever from cat bites."

Well, another crisis in the life of Jasmine. Incidentally, the tiny catnip pillow is now on the living room floor and she completely ignores it. Maybe she is still recovering from the trauma of the incident. I know that I am.

When I told my cousin about the incident, she said, "Oh, no, is Jasmine all right?" I felt it necessary to point out to her in the nicest possible way, that perhaps she should be concerned about her cousin, not the cat.

MARK 10:19—*Thou knowest the commandments: Do not commit adultery; Do not kill; Do not steal; Do not bear false witness; Defraud not; Honor thy father and mother.*

Chapter 45

While the announcement was made some time ago of the retirement of R. Terry Brownell as superintendent of our schools, I always operate on the theory that if one ignores something unpleasant, it just might go away. However, that hasn't proved true in this case, and Mr. Brownell is going to retire.

In his more than thirty years with us, he won the admiration and respect of his students, the faculty, other school personnel and our communities. He has remarkable qualities which few possess, and which many of us envy. His intelligent, calm approach to the most controversial issues.—That indefinable trait that gains him the respect of the students, while yet conveying to them the knowledge that he is approachable.—The combination of his dignity, and yet his friendliness.—His open-minded, fair approach to all issues. I have personally seen him handle some touchy situations with understanding and fairness, displaying an open-minded, calm attitude. How often he has turned a delicate situation into just another passing incident with the correct phrase!

He is well-known among school administrators throughout the state for his knowledge of school affairs—financing, grants, legislation and problem areas. He has coped admirably well with all of them. Knowledgeable and intelligent, he has often dealt with people who are poorly informed on the complexities of school administration, and yet he listens to their suggestions and criticisms with patience and forbearance. Most of us would be tempted to set them straight in no uncertain terms, but his tact and diplomacy are apparently boundless.

We can't forget his wife, June, since both of them have endeared themselves to the community. Mrs. Brownell has also won our admiration and respect. Both Mr. and Mrs. Brownell have been active in church affairs, he being an elder and Clerk of Sessions for many years, and she being an officer and active member of the women's group. Mr. Brownell is also active in the Lions Club and the Historical Society, while his wife is deeply involved in the projects of the Women's Club.

"Pillars of the community" might be a little trite, but what better phrase would one find to describe this remarkable couple? "We'll miss them" is the understatement of all time!

Both Mr. Brownell and his wife have since passed away, leaving a void in our community that never can be filled.

MATTHEW 22:37—*Jesus said unto him, Thou shalt love the Lord, thy God, with all thy heart, and with all thy soul, and with all thy mind.*

Chapter 46

Local deer hunters have been "getting in the mood" this week. This deer hunting preparation is a mighty serious business. First, comes the search for the red or blaze orange clothing. Whether it is ten years old, or just purchased, the colorful attire must apparently be "broken in" by wearing it for at least a week prior to the opening of season. Next in line for attention is the trusty rifle, which has been stored since last deer season. However, rifles must be in constant danger of some terrible "rifle affliction," because the gun receives a most studied scrutiny, as though some dangerous malady could have attacked it while it was resting safely in storage.

Some time during the week, the members of the hunting party find time to visit "the shack" where they will be staying during the season. The dust and dirt in the shack are rearranged, and an ample supply of wood is gathered, with the thought (or hope) in mind that the entire hunting party might get snowbound and have to stay an extra week (let it snow, let it snow, let it snow). After the cords of wood are placed at a convenient spot near the door, the kerosene and fuel oil supply is checked, and other similar tasks are completed.

Now comes the "social hour," during which the prospective hunters sit around the fire at the shack, drinking coffee (and other stronger liquids) and repeating the stories of every deer kill they have ever made. In the case of older hunters, with far more deer to their credit, this "social hour" could extend into a couple of days, and they usually decide to spend the couple of days before season right at the shack.

Most deer hunters are of the male species, so the next step in the preparation is taken with a great deal of enthusiasm—the compiling of the grocery list. Men who are helpless when faced with a frying pan and an egg, now deliriously plan exotic meals of pheasant under glass, potatoes au gratin and baked Alaska. Baked turkey banquets are planned with carefree abandon, and wives stand drooling as the grocery list lengthens and the dishes become more and more complicated. The tons of food are packed into boxes several days ahead of time, with the purchase of the perishables scheduled for the last minute.

Things are pretty much under control, and the restless, would-be hunter can now settle down to details—securing his license, rounding up boots, sox, heavy underwear, etc. A visit to the sporting goods store to purchase the shells is good for a couple of hours' time, since he is certain to meet another hunter, intent on the same purpose, and more deer are verbally killed, with the weather also discussed at great length.

It is about now that the little woman comes up with an ultimatum. Suddenly, she remembers a too-long-postponed chore around the house, and the happy, carefree hunter is knocked clear out of his trance by his shrewd frau, who decides that "Either that bedroom gets painted before you leave, or you're JUST NOT GOING." Many are the reactions to this type of statement, but if a member of the fairer sex thinks for even a second that anything short of an act of God could keep her hunter home, she can only be a new bride, experiencing her first year at having her hubby going hunting.

Everyone has been alerted as to the hour of departure, every possible detail has been ironed out, items to be packed are standing in untidy heaps and now the pacing begins, as the hunter travels from window to window, awaiting the arrival of "the fellows." This waiting period is never long, since all the men are equally anxious to get away, and an hour or two before the specified time, the red-clad buddies arrive, and with one "woosh" the joyous hunters, laden with bag and baggage, swoop out the door, laughing uproariously at nothing at all.

GENESIS 10:9—*He was a mighty hunter before the Lord; wherefore it is said, Even as Nimrod the mighty hunter before the Lord.*

Chapter 47

Picture this, if you will. You're driving home from work. It is very cold and very dark. The wind is whipping snow across the road. You're hungry. You're cold. It has been a busy day.

At home, you're greeted by a husband who wants his supper and a dog who wants attention. A dog who, unlike his mother, does not believe in procrastination. He immediately reminds you that after dinner he wants to go for a walk, and please HURRY! Let's say the dog is glad to see you. He's hungry, too.

As the dinner is taken out to thaw in the microwave, you look through the mail. Glaring out from among the junk mail is a message. "GOODBYE! Mrs. Burgess. I thought we were friends."

I won't go into the embarrassing details of the message. I am rude. I am crude. I am entirely lacking in the social graces—in fact, I wouldn't know a social grace if I saw one. I am a "taker," never a "giver." I am a blight on society—a pimple on the face of perfection.

Where did I go wrong, Mary? What happened to our beautiful relationship of just a few short months ago (the months are, indeed, short, aren't they)? I am the very same person to whom you wrote, "We love you, Mrs. Burgess." I thought at the time that "love" was a mighty strong word, but I accepted your statement, because it was so flattering. (I can't find too many people who even "like" me! As a matter of fact, have you heard the expression, "a person that only a mother could love?") You loved me so much you wanted to give me a million dollars! Now this. Are you really the same Mary Ann Spencer?

Mary Ann is hurt and angry. For years I have had the gall to accept the catalogs which she so generously mails to me, and not once have I had the decency to place an order.

But wait. I might be an outcast, a boor, a greedy, insensitive slob. Someone is willing to forgive all of it and wants to meet me?? I check the address to make certain the message is really for me. Nobody has ever, ever expressed a desire to meet me. "How are we ever going to meet unless you are the one million dollar winner? All I'm asking, Mrs. Burgess, is that at least you give me and yourself an opportunity to meet." This message isn't from Mary Ann. None other than Art Linkletter added a postscript to Mary Ann's letter. Art Linkletter wants to meet ME? Mary Ann should have read his message before she sent me the caustic note. I'll bet Art Linkletter has never written to her, expressing an ardent desire to meet HER. However, as I continue to read his message, I begin to wonder about him. Isn't he a married man? "Certainly Mrs. Walls and I will never forget the time we spent together," he wrote, referring to the wonderful occasion when it brought him immeasurable happiness to present a cash prize to the winning Mrs. Walls. If his generosity brings him so much happiness, I suppose I'll have to take my million dollars. What are friends for? I wasn't even aware I was a friend of Art, but even if he were an enemy, I wouldn't refuse his million dollars. I can tell by his letter that he is a most discriminating person who recognizes when someone is truly outstanding, in spite of what Mary Ann says.

I read on. Wouldn't you know? There's a catch to all this. Art is going to give me a million dollars all right. There's no doubt about that. There it is, in black and white. In fact, he is just dying to present me the money. HOWEVER—the clincher is in the "bottom line," as they say. (It really was the bottom line, too.) I am to get only a paltry $50,000.00 a year. The million is to be spread over annual payments for twenty years. Does Art know how old I am? What good is $50,000.00 going to do me when I'm a hundred years old?

As I mentally work on negotiations with Art to get my million dollars during a far shorter period of time, I begin to thaw more dinners. Jim wants to eat. Bucky wants to eat NOW. I have to wash a batch of clothes. When I get my million dollars, I'll never wash clothes again. I'll just throw the dirty clothes away.

I'll have to get in touch with Art tomorrow.

PROVERBS 22:2—*The rich and poor meet together; the Lord is the maker of them all.*

Chapter 48

My moment of triumph was very fleeting, but while it lasted I didn't hesitate to bask in the praise of my gardening skill. Call it hypocritical if you will (as, indeed, you rightfully should) but the fact remains that this beautiful, exotic plant WAS in MY garden. Since everything I know about gardening could be written on the head of one small pin, all plants growing in my garden must reach maturity before any weeding can be done. This has resulted, year after year, with a crop of strong, sturdy, healthy weeds choking out a few sickly, struggling flowers. This year is no exception, other than the fact that the condition is intensified, it seems.

A month or so ago, amidst the weeds, sprouted a suspicious-looking plant. (Frankly, everything in my garden looks questionable.) For once, my lackadaisical attitude towards gardening paid off, because the plant flourished, grew tall and sturdy, and to everyone's astonishment, started to flower. The flowers were gorgeous. This is a fact—I swear—complete strangers would stop at the office to ask what kind of plant it was. Having to tell them that I had no idea took a little wind out of my sails, I'll admit, but I would let nothing ruin my moment of glory. Then, the plant was identified. Friends informed me that I had the most beautiful columbine they had ever seen!

Well, pride goeth before a fall, all right. The plant became laden with huge blossoms, and more and more buds were in evidence. I took pictures, I boasted, I began to think of myself as a botanist, rather than a gardener. And, now to the sad ending. One evening a little dog got into my garden, and as I attempted to shoo him out he fearfully darted to the far corner and broke off my beautiful plant. I stood holding the gorgeous plant, stunned at the tragic turn of events, which again reduced me to the status of a would-be gardener. I do have a photo of the columbine, but will I ever be able to convince readers that this breathtaking plant was in my garden? I doubt it.

So I am again humbled and have received my "just dues." Now I will confess. That plant grew by sheer accident. A houseplant which had been given to me during the winter met the same fate as all my plants—it died within a very short time. This spring I threw the pot of earth out into the garden, and it was from this little mound of earth (which, through negligence, I had not even leveled off) that this beautiful plant sprouted. They say confession is good for the soul, but somehow, I still don't feel very good about that little dog breaking by beautiful plant, although I realize now that I was getting far too big-headed about what I had deceitfully termed "my gardening skill."

MATTHEW 7:1—*Judge not, that ye be not judged.*

Chapter 49

I will not tell you the name of our telephone company, but if it does not get its act together soon, I will divulge its identity. My telephone bill for August indicated a $45.32 credit. What a lovely present, but I felt that I should notify the company of its error. After I pressed numbers on the telephone for an interminably long time and was transferred to three different people, one of whom hinted that it was all my fault, I was assured that the error (THEIRS) would be corrected. I told one of the telephone people that the credit was very generous of them, and I certainly was not complaining—but . . . I had spent almost an hour on the telephone. I sent in a check for our usual monthly fee.

In September, my credit was increased by one penny; it was now $45.33. I went through the whole procedure again. The numbers, the music, the hype for all the services the company offers. I got the feeling that this company never makes a mistake and if there is a discrepancy, "WE" know who is to blame. With a sigh, the woman assured me that it would be corrected, and her tone carried a note of disgust for anyone who would complain about a credit. I sent in the usual monthly fee.

Well, the company took care of its error in grand style. My October bill showed that I owed them $171.92! Whine about a credit?

They showed me! I did the telephone numbers, listened to the "press 1 for this, press 2 for that—up to 9," the hype, the music, the taped statements of satisfied customers who had received a free computer from the telephone company and were in Seventh Heaven. I was referred to three of their personnel, passing the buck, and after an hour, when the third one had me on "hold" for over fifteen minutes, I hung up, knowing I would have to go through the whole dreary procedure again. The next day, which was as soon as I could gain back my strength for another call, I got a young man, Brian, who listened to my tale of woe and after another forty-five minutes, assured me that adjustments would be made and "everything would be all right" by the time my next bill arrived. He sounded so convincing! I again sent in a check for my usual monthly fee.

Now, we come to my November bill. True to his word, Brian had "taken care of it." I now owed only $160.46! Here we go again. I knew the routine so well by this time. Numbers, music, hype, thrilled telephone customers who got free computers and could not now live without them. Finally I got Sue, who was sympathetic to my situation. She explained that when a customer pays online and presses one number wrong, it could create just such a situation. It happened to her once with another firm. We visited (she is having major surgery in January). Then she put me on "hold" while she conferred with Brian. Back on the line, she said that Brian had sent his greetings, and I stated that Brian was not on my list of favorite people at the moment because he had promised—PROMISED—that my financial situation with the telephone company would definitely be resolved before the next billing. She and Brian had the situation under control and my next statement would be for the correct amount. In the spirit of Christmas, I wished Brian and Sue a Merry Christmas, and sent in my usual monthly fee.

The dreary saga continued on Monday, December 24—what a nice Christmas present. A "Past Due Notice." "If payment is not received by 4:30 on the final due date (January 3, 2008) your service will be temporarily disconnected without further notice. . . . If your services are discontinued, you will pay $28.00 before your telephone service will be turned on again." It is the day before Christmas and it is extremely busy at The News office. The next chapter cannot be written until Thursday, December 27—and January 3 is approaching at an alarming rate. I have this premonition that even if it is not my fault, and the service is discontinued, I will still owe the $28.00.

IS THERE NO END TO THIS STORY?

A number of people keep calling my home to see if I still have telephone service. I do, but not because I paid the $160.46 that we were billed. I wrote in this column at length a couple of weeks ago about my longstanding disagreement with our telephone company, whose bills since August have been incorrect.

At the advice of a friend (thanks so much, Irv) I wrote to the Public Utilities Commission and included a copy of the Chaos column and copies of our phone bills. I also sent all this material to the Attorney General's office. Well, the ink had scarcely dried on my signature on the letter before I got a reply from the Public Utilities Commission. . . .

"Thank you for contacting the Commission with your concerns. The Commission has contacted - - - - - and investigated your billing concerns. - - - - - found payments have been misapplied on behalf of the company. The company recognized their error in billing and service. According to - - - - - your current balance is $1.52 and your future statements will be correctly billed at $26.36 per month. Please feel free to contact - - - - - and the Commission if you have any further concerns. Thank you for contacting the Commission."

What prompt action! Kudos to the Public Utilities Commission. You are great people.

I do feel uncomfortable about the $1.52 bill (I can just hear readers sighing, "Good heavens, is she not ever satisfied?") I really do owe them $26.36, but if I paid that amount, this entire farce would go on for another six or eight months. I am sending the $1.52

The following day, I received a communication from the Attorney General, whose letter was lengthy and read more like a legal document. The Consumer Services Division of the Office of the Attorney General advised that it has limited authority and cannot provide legal advice to private citizens. It did, however, offer some comments and said that it had been in contact with the telephone company.

I do hope this is the end of the "Telephone Bill Saga." At the moment, all is well, but the next telephone bill will tell the story. I have nothing but admiration for the Attorney General's office and the Minnesota Public Utilities Commission. They both addressed my problem immediately and seem to get results. I do not want to sound pessimistic; but I will have to wait for my telephone bill before I can really breathe a sigh of relief.

I, too, thought each month for five months that I had the problem solved by myself, and each month a representative of the telephone company assured me that my next bill would reflect the correct amount that I owed. Foolish me to be taken in so easily!

My telephone bill came in the mail on Thursday. This was the bill which would decide if my problems with the telephone company were resolved. I literally tore the envelope apart, even got a paper cut on my finger in my haste. There it was, worthy of framing! My bill for the correct amount. That is the end of the story—and what a happy ending!

ROMANS 15:13—*Now the God of hope fill you with all joy and peace in believing, that ye may abound in hope, through the power of the Holy Spirit.*

Chapter 50

No matter how I condition myself to making the telephone call, I am completely intimidated by having my call answered by "a recording." I know of several area businesses which use these recording devices, and even when I am aware of the fact that my call might be answered by "This is a recording," I never can cope with it when it happens. My first impulse is to childishly hang up without saying a word. That is what I really want to do. However, in confusion, I manage to remember my name and my tongue trips over the syllables as I identify myself, thereby committing myself to what I feel is the downright embarrassing situation of talking to that recorder "at the sound of the tone." Foreseeing the possibility of encountering such a predicament, in advance I carefully prepare my "speech" for that recorder, with its superior air. No amount of preparation can solve my dilemma of trying to fill that void of silence with my stumbling, stuttering message.

Of course, nobody is able to make sense out of my recorded messages, other than to get my name. As I end the "speech," I am faced with another problem. Does one say "good-bye" to the recorder or just hang up? It seems rude to hang up without some phrase of farewell. I've ended my monologue with "That's it then," "O.K?" or "Did you get that?" all of which are mighty unsophisticated—but what can you expect from such an unsophisticated person?

The other recordings which pose a problem for me are the messages from the telephone company, after I've dialed a number. I know all of those recordings by heart (my memory being what it is, that is a miracle in itself), but it seems so rude, crude and unkind to hang up in the middle of the recording. I know it is ridiculous, and I feel like a fool "hanging in there" for the entire message, but I just can't bring myself to hang up the receiver.

There is no doubt about it—I was definitely born one hundred years too late!

MATTHEW 11:28—*Come unto me, all ye that labor and are heavy laden, and I will give you rest.*

About the Author

Phyllis Driscoll entered the weekly newspaper field when she married the publisher of a small weekly newspaper, Franklin J. "Jim" Burgess, in Tower, Minnesota. During the past sixty years, she has seen the newspaper publishing business through its may stages. Jim had a modern shop for its time- a linotype, job press, newspaper press and countless cases of type which had to be handset. The weekly editions of *The Tower News* had to be folded by hand and addressed by cutting and pasting the address labels onto each copy. However, Jim was never one to accept status quo; he advocated progress and constantly (maddeningly) continued throughout his years as publisher to keep abreast of the most up-to-date equipment in the small weekly newspaper field. He was diligent and dedicated. He actually seemed driven.

Phyllis eased into the business gradually, learning one phase after another, always having to be prodded because she lacked—make that lacks—confidence. She eventually learned to operate each new piece of equipment, except, to Jim's consternation, the art of "feeding the press." Meeting a pressman with a hook for a hand (because he did not move his hand quickly enough when "feeding the press") did nothing to boost her confidence. Always keeping up with the times, Jim eventually "went offset," as the publishers used to say, and his newspaper was eventually printed at a central plant. It is of no significance to anyone but Phyllis (and is not known to anyone else except those at this reading) but she is proud of the fact that she is the only one in the newspaper's more than a century of existence who put out an issue of the paper single-handedly while Jim was at Mayo Clinic for a week. She acknowledges that it took long nightly telephone conversations with Jim to make it possible.

Phyllis still works at *The Tower News* three days a week. Jim retired in 1980 and died in 2006. She has a daughter and son-in-law, Pat and Paul, who reside in Duluth.